Set Free

The Authentic Catholic Woman's
Guide to Forgiveness

GENEVIEVE KINEKE

SERVANT
BOOKS

PUBLISHED BY FRANCISCAN MEDIA
Cincinnati, Ohio

Cover and book design by Mark Sullivan
Cover image © PhotoXpress | waterlilly

LIBRARY OF CONGRESS CATALOGING-IN-PUBLICATION DATA
Kineke, Genevieve S., 1960-
Set free : the authentic Catholic woman›s guide to forgiveness / Genevieve Kineke.
p. cm.
Includes bibliographical references.
ISBN 978-1-61636-489-2 (alk. paper)
1. Catholic women—Religious life. 2. Forgiveness—Religious aspects—Catholic Church. 3. Love—Religious aspects—Catholic Church. I. Title.
BX2353.K565 2012
248.8'43088282—dc23
2012030392

Published by Servant Books, an imprint of Franciscan Media
28 W. Liberty St.
Cincinnati, OH 45202
www.ServantBooks.org
www.FranciscanMedia.org

Printed in the United States of America.
Printed on acid-free paper.
12 13 14 15 16 5 4 3 2 1

For B.D.
who showed me how

• • •

CONTENTS

It happened earlier this year, in unfamiliar territory, while I was on my way to celebrate the funeral of a friend. Recently it happened again, this time on a familiar road, while I was on my way to a well-known and beloved chapel. Despite good intentions and careful planning, my journey was suddenly interrupted, brought to a standstill by a formidable sign in the middle of the road: BRIDGE CLOSED.

Bridges often provide the surest way to arrive at our destination, and sometimes bridges may be the only way. But imagine a world in which many of those bridges are broken or in disrepair. Think of all the beautiful places and deeply personal spaces that would remain forever uncharted, undiscovered, and unknown.

In her previous book, *The Authentic Catholic Woman*, Genevieve Kineke describes with brilliance the vocation of woman as icon of the Church, called to image the Bride of Christ in all her splendor through everyday living and total self-giving. I enjoyed that work thoroughly, since I was able to benefit from this fruitful perspective not only as a reader but also because, at the time, I was her parish priest. In this richly theological and disarmingly personal book, *Set Free: The Authentic Catholic Woman's Guide to Forgiveness*, Genevieve enunciates anew that call of woman to be, like Holy Mother Church, a bridge facilitating reconciliation between fathers and children, and between God and all of creation.

In a fallen world, however, bridges get burned, and promises are broken. When women are wounded and their souls have sustained seemingly irreparable damage, what becomes of the hope that their vocation will "aid mankind in not falling"[1] and the promise they hold for a world thirsting for reconciliation and love? Brokenness, suffering, and pain appear to be in direct contrast to so lofty a calling, but in such a state she begins to resemble more and more completely her Spouse.

Set Free reminds us that the vocation of women is not necessarily hindered by the crosses of life—whether betrayal, abuse, neglect, or a host of other injuries—but that even there can be found the seeds of healing and hope. The wedding chamber where the Divine Bridegroom is united to his Bride in this world is revealed as the wood of the cross, and here is a union that is difficult and mysterious but at the same time most fruitful. "We find ourselves at the heart of the Paschal Mystery," writes Pope John Paul II, "which completely reveals the spousal love of God. Christ is the Bridegroom because 'he has given himself': his body has been 'given,' his blood has been 'poured out'.... The 'sincere gift' contained in the sacrifice of the Cross gives definitive prominence to the spousal meaning of God's love."[2] Our late Holy Father goes on to describe this union in the Eucharist, the Sacrament of our Redemption and the Sacrament of Bridegroom and Bride.[3] What Genevieve proposes in these pages is that the Bride has something significant to give back to God and to the world: her reception of Christ's gift and then the sincere gift of herself in forgiving and loving in a courageously feminine way. I have witnessed firsthand this remarkable self-gift in the author herself, and I am profoundly grateful that she has answered the call of God to perpetuate that gift with this book.

In the Introduction, Genevieve describes forgiveness as the universal path to wisdom and the only reliable passage to true freedom and ineffable joy. I am sure that as you read the remarkable stories of women who have made that arduous but liberating journey from injury to forgiveness you will understand why. By the wood of the cross, Christ was able to build for us a way home to the Father; even so does the power of forgiveness begin to repair the bridges of our fallen world, and the dignity and vocation of women stands stronger and is illumined brilliantly once again.

How desperately the world we live in longs for this vocation, desires this self-gift of every woman! How central to woman's happiness and fulfillment, Genevieve contends, is the accomplishment of this mission. But it must begin with the grace of being forgiven and then find its consummation in the heart of the lover set free to imitate her Spouse. There is no magic formula for forgiveness, however, no quick fix. Instead, Genevieve provides some practical dimensions and follows this with everyday experiences of women who have suffered at the hands of fathers, mothers, and children; sustained injuries by members of the Church, by abortion, by oneself, or by the world at large. "I will run in the way of your commandments," writes the psalmist, "when you enlarge my understanding" (Psalm 119:32). These stories will become a wellspring of grace for the wounded soul who longs for healing and will open up pathways to freedom for those who have been bound by bitterness and regret.

This book is not an autobiography, but by all means it is a personal journey to the heart of forgiveness and the mercy of God. When Genevieve speaks of letting go and giving back to

God all that he has given us, when she writes of the transformation and renewal that comes about through an all-encompassing maternity and spousal union with God, she is not merely theologizing. Clearly she is speaking from experience as mother, as bride, as woman. From this personal perspective she asks: "Can we create bridges of communion by casting off the evil that seeks to isolate each soul in darkness?"

That is a question that can only be answered personally, perhaps even painfully, but never is it a question answered alone. The Divine Bridegroom, who gives himself to us in the Sacrament of the Eucharist and comes to us in our deepest need, begins to restore what we never intended to lose and to repair what has been broken and damaged by sin. By ourselves, such restoration and the ability to forgive may be impossible, but for God, all things are possible and building bridges is his forte. Dear reader, may the pages of this book set you free to become the beautiful gift that you are to the world, and may your happiness, your greatest joy, be rediscovered in the dignity and vocation that is yours alone.

Rev. Christopher M. Mahar
Rector, Seminary of Our Lady of Providence

Women are usually full of advice. From parenting tips to fashion commentary—and everything in between—our opinions are plentiful. Whether we share them or not, they are on parade in our heads as we make our way in the world. Rare is the day when we haven't thought firmly to ourselves, "She ought to…"

But as many answers as I once thought I had, I admit that I'm really brought up short when someone actually looks me in the eye and says, "What do *you* think I should do?" And as rare as those moments are when someone sincerely solicits an opinion, I'm finding it harder and harder to answer. As the years pile up, my new mantra has become "The more I know, the less I know." Truly!

Life is complex; there are many moving parts. Families, especially, are a conglomerate of diverse personalities who seem to face a never-ending list of challenges. Memories are long, gossip muddies the waters, there are financial realities to be faced, and so often we miss the mark in terms of patience and charity. We hear the gospel command to love one another, but is that realistic, considering how complicated things get? And could God really be serious about loving *these* people? Doesn't he understand how hard it is?

Well, yes, he does. If you'll recall, Jesus himself was exasperated at times. When asked by one set of parents to heal their boy who was possessed by a demon, he answered, "O faithless and perverse generation, how long am I to be with you? How long am I to bear with you?" (Matthew 17:17). And when he was poised to heal the man with a withered hand, "he looked around at [the men of the synagogue] with anger, grieved at their hardness of heart" (Mark 3:5). And surely their obstinacy and lack of faith were little compared to their final rejection of his love— the rejection that led to his tortured and bloody death. Still he insisted on love, for that was who he was. It was his nature, his very essence and his gift to those who share his likeness.

So how do we make the leap from the messy shortcomings of everyday life to the paradise Jesus offers? The same way that he did—through forgiveness. Just as he forgave the lash and the nails, the thorns and the jeers, we must forgive all who have hurt us in any way. In the Sermon on the Mount, Jesus taught his followers how to pray and explained: "For if you forgive men their trespasses, your heavenly Father also will forgive you; but if you do not forgive men their trespasses, neither will your Father forgive your trespasses" (Matthew 6:14–15).

So although I have let go of many of my opinions concerning mundane things—especially those that concern the lives of others—I have become more firmly convinced than ever that forgiveness is the universal path to wisdom and the only reliable passage to freedom and joy. I have found through years of presentations on the topic that the actual mechanics of the process can be bewildering to those faced with deeply personal wounds, especially wounds that have festered for decades. I hope that this book will help clarify the way.

Trust me, trust those who share their stories of forgiveness in this book, and trust God himself, whose unfathomable love for us is magnified in his divine mercy. This is advice you can rely upon. Truly!

CHAPTER ONE

The Feminine Vocation

In *The Authentic Catholic Woman*, I outlined the feminine vocation using the Church as a concrete template. In order to understand how that is possible, we must first understand that there are two dimensions of that one institution.

When many think of the Church, they think of the pope, bishops, and priests who make up the hierarchy. These successors of the apostles, who administer the sacraments and govern with the authority vested in them by Christ himself, make up what we call the Petrine Church, which can be likened to a bridegroom. They exercise headship over the family of God, planting the Word (*semen*) and safeguarding its growth. As *alter Christi*, each man is called to lay down his life for the benefit of those in his care, just as Our Lord did.

But that is only one way to look at the Church. There is also the image of the Marian Church, the mystical bride whose union with the Bridegroom bears spiritual children for the kingdom of God. Holy Mother Church—born from the pierced side of Christ after he was crushed for our offenses—carries forward the Incarnation by making his truth known and loved among all peoples. Her motherly mantle enfolds all who profess this truth and provides a sanctuary of love amid the trials of the world.

While there are other illustrative images of the Church throughout Scripture, these two are the most comprehensive, and between them they reveal the nuptial love that God has for his people. There is no contradiction or rivalry between these two dimensions; rather they work together on behalf of the same mission and carry us in their supernatural embrace.

Obviously, those who are feminine are privileged in a particular way to live as icons of the Marian Church—virgin, bride, and mother—and that is where we find the essence of our vocation. In concrete terms, this means that we are called to mirror the sacramental realities according to the circumstances of our lives: for example, healing, teaching, creating culture, reconciling, and mothering. In a word, we love—by receiving the love of the Bridegroom in our maternal hearts and sharing it with others.

Authentic femininity encompasses our call to live out a spiritual motherhood upon which the world depends. Each woman makes this motherhood uniquely her own according to her talents and opportunities but primarily through a judicious response to those who depend on her—including her family, friends, and coworkers. It is essential that she understand the complementarity between men and women and how authentic masculinity and femininity are each integral to the formation of healthy families and a stable society. Finally, all of her activities should be grounded in prayer and guided by a mature view of human nature.

To Love in a Fallen World Means to Suffer

Unfortunately, anyone familiar with this world knows that loving others is a difficult task. The best of intentions are often misunderstood, communicating effectively can be a challenge, our defects and the defects of others collide in the most disastrous ways—and then there is the sad reality that many people with whom we come into contact have no desire to live virtue or to love others.

Against this backdrop, people hurt others on a regular basis—both through their actions and in failing to act. Some injuries are caused by the deliberate ill will of others, which can be either premeditated or spontaneous; some are due to negligence or poor judgment, since we don't always think through our words or actions; some may be the result of chance, the unfortunate alignment of events that seem outside anyone's control; and then there are those efforts meant to be kind or helpful that don't go over well or that others interpret badly. Almost anyone's life could reveal a litany of injuries from the earliest years—with many causing pain and the worst leading to alienation and the inability to love.

While some elements of personal and societal suffering are timeless, our generation is undergoing a particular deconstruction that is grievously disorienting. Many marriages are fragile and unstable, and thus society's customary bedrock is crumbling, causing increasing numbers of young people to shy away from the institution entirely. Those who do understand its foundational mission are vastly outnumbered by those who have little interest in promoting the virtues necessary to its survival.

For a variety of reasons, many of our elderly are alone or in institutions, and many young people have embraced materialism and promiscuity in the hope of masking their deep loneliness. Since the wider society is both exacerbating and reacting to the confused approach to natural law, our legal system is no longer oriented to the good of persons—especially children. Thus there are few sanctuaries that can truly shelter human persons and introduce them to the love for which they were created.

The sexual revolution in particular has had a devastating effect, though many are still unwilling to admit it. Those who have prayerfully considered the facts, though, realize that widespread acceptance of contraception has contributed to broken marriages, the mainstreaming of promiscuity and cohabitation, staggering abortion rates, and pervasive public vulgarity. Growing numbers of parents and teachers have been either unwilling or unable to model virtue for their children, and women are realizing that they've been objectified from an early age—even by those charged with safeguarding them.

Although each of these trends can be dissected and analyzed in broad sociological terms, the pain is not abstract—*each injury is deeply personal.* One can point to the fact that roughly half of marriages fail in the United States, but that statistic has little bearing on the fact that *your* husband left you or that *your* parents no longer share a home. Likewise, the fact that most third-grade girls cannot keep secrets is no comfort when *your* deepest confidence has been betrayed. Behind each statistic is at least one wounded soul—and usually more than one.

Choosing to Love

While the last century has created some unique contexts that are particularly challenging to women, it is important to remember that all generations have suffered since turning away from God. And thus—like all God's children—we are called to return to him and be consoled, to walk in his paths of love.

Surely the logical, mundane response to suffering is to refuse to love. Whether because of dysfunction within the family or unfortunate encounters with others, many girls learn early in life to protect their hearts by limiting their generosity. They set up a host of inconsistent boundaries that have less to do with virtue than with survival. Even in intimate encounters and within their families, many are afraid to give a complete gift of self. Through this very caution they cut themselves off from the only guaranteed avenue of happiness. Their need for love and stability doesn't diminish; their greatest desires are thwarted by confusion over where and how to expend their energy, and each step in their disordered search for intimacy only deepens the spiral of pain.

The crux of the matter is that man and woman are both called to generous love, to complete gifts of self, but precisely because women are icons of the Church—the paradigm of the feminine responsiveness that ultimately includes all of creation—they must be first to model this love. Pope John Paul II wrote in his apostolic letter "On the Dignity and Vocation of Women":

> "Man, who is the only creature on earth that God willed for its own sake, cannot fully find himself except through a sincere gift of self." This applies to every human being, as a person created in God's image, whether man or woman. This ontological affirmation also indicates the ethical dimension of a person's vocation. *Woman can only find herself by giving love to others.*[4]

That means that, despite the fallen world, despite their particular vulnerabilities, and despite the pain involved, it is essential that women persevere in love. They must love for two reasons: The world needs their love, and their own happiness depends upon it. Who but women have been invited to receive human persons and to form them through the multifaceted gift of motherhood?

The fact that the spiritual and emotional health of each woman has a profound rippling effect on the wider culture cannot be overstated. It is for this very reason that there was an urgent call to women included in the Closing Documents of the Second Vatican Council: "[A]t this moment when the human race is under-going so deep a transformation, women impregnated with the spirit of the Gospel can do so much to aid mankind in not falling."[5]

So what does the "spirit of the Gospel" tell us about loving in a fallen world? The answer is clear: We are to forgive the injuries and love those who have harmed us. The Bridegroom himself came in love and was crucified, and his last words were words of forgiveness (see Luke 23:34, 43). As icons of his beloved bride, we have no other option, despite the staggering implications of such a demand.

What could God be thinking? What does he actually mean by forgiveness? How is it done? Is it even possible when the wounds run deep? And what is the point, when many of these things happened so long ago? All of these questions will be addressed as we continue.

The Martyrs of Forgiveness

Just as our faith in Christ depends on the eyewitness accounts of his resurrection, our ability to forgive is helped along by hearing the details of how others have done it. Just as each Christian martyr (meaning "witness") was willing to testify to the truth about God no matter what, the martyrs of forgiveness boldly attest to the truth of Our Lord's instruction to imitate his own definitive pardon. When we see these people of faith who have progressed beyond a grim, white-knuckled acceptance of God's permissive will—finding not only peace but transforming joy—we know that the counterintuitive admonishment to forgive is an unfailing corridor of healing and restoration, which is what Jesus ardently wants for each of us.

Ultimately, the greatest example we have of strictly human forgiveness is the Blessed Mother, who also stands as the most perfect icon of the Church. Her spiritual motherhood was forged at the height of her suffering, when her tortured son looked down and asked her to embrace the same sinful humanity that put him there. Previously, when presenting this beloved child in the temple, she had been warned that her own soul would be pierced (see Luke 2:35), and here it came to pass. Her suffocating grief discovered a vent in an expanded motherhood founded on forgiveness—*and we entered in.* With her heart worn raw and eyes burning with tears, she took all humanity to her bosom.

This work of forgiveness, then, is integral to our feminine vocation. It will not only transform each of us but also give new life to the Church, through which humanity will be reconciled to its loving Father. Not only will we "aid humanity in not falling," but we can provide a bridge of healing and restoration for others at this critical juncture. Who could not undertake this important work, when Jesus said so clearly, so convincingly, and so often, "Be not afraid!" (see Matthew 10:19, 31; Mark 6:50; Luke 8:50; John 14:27).

CHAPTER TWO

Love Stands in the Breach

In order to understand the relationship between any offense and the need for forgiveness, one must begin by understanding sin and grace. For this we begin by thinking about God, who alone is entirely good. He is perfectly good, not only because he is a perfect being but because he is "goodness" and "being" itself. Our being and the being of all creation depend on him, and any good that we find is but a shadow or sliver of his very essence.

The Nature of Sin

Given the nature of our goodness and the goodness we see all around us, we must then consider what is missing when we fail to be good. That deficiency is called sin, which is the Latin word for "without." The action that is deprived of God's being or essence lacks goodness and constitutes a moral deprivation that we call sin.

Since God is all good, there is no deficiency in him, and nothing sinful can come from him. But it is obvious that there is sin in the world, so the driving question has always been to discover where it originated. The Christian explanation is that when God created man in his own image—"male and female he created them" (Genesis 1:27)—he shared with them two key qualities of his own nature: his goodness and his freedom. Unfortunately, human beings abused the freedom with which God endowed them. Instead of using it to choose the good without coercion or encumbrances, our first parents chose that which was opposed to the good. In that pivotal choice they bequeathed original sin to all subsequent generations.

But God—who was rejected in this choice—chose to respond in mercy. Instead of condemning his creation to destruction, he promised to restore the ruptured relationship. Thousands of years of anticipation over this promise was met with two astonishing revelations: First, the singular God of Abraham, Isaac, and Jacob was actually three divine persons in one; and second, the promised Messiah was none other than God himself, taking flesh from the Virgin Mary.

Understanding both the Trinity and the Incarnation is integral to understanding God's forgiveness of our sins (inasmuch as we can understand such things). The gravity of sin depends on two things—the seriousness of the offense and the one whom it offends. When a person defies God, his sin is that much more disgraceful because he has insulted the all-good Creator who has gratuitously given him everything. Moreover, since all persons are made in the image and likeness of God, when we offend our neighbor, we offend God who resides in him. Furthermore, since God is in us as well, when we fail to do the right thing, we sin against him living in our person.

Just as it seems that this threefold mirror (God, neighbor, and self) has surrounded us and magnified our errors beyond repair, that same extraordinary combination of the Trinity and the Incarnation comes to our rescue to make redemption possible.

Since God is offended in each sin, only a divine sacrifice will repair the breach that sin has brought about.

> For in him all the fulness of God was pleased to dwell, and through him to reconcile to himself all things, whether on earth or in heaven, making peace by the blood of his cross. (Colossians 1:19–20)

Since Jesus is the Second Person of the Trinity, it follows that the gift he offers—laying down his life in atonement for our sins—is God rendered up to God as the only acceptable sacrifice: "In Christ God was reconciling the world to himself" (2 Corinthians 5:19). And since that divine sacrifice was made in the form of one who was entirely human—like us in all things but sin—he carries us, flesh of his flesh, in himself along the road to Calvary, restoring dignity to our tarnished likeness.

Finally, in responding to his appalling treatment by forgiving his tormenters, Jesus revealed to us the singular path to freedom. This is what John Paul II expressed in *Dives in Misericordia*:

> ...[W]e must note that Christ, in revealing the love-mercy of God, at the same time demanded from people that they also should be guided in their lives by love and mercy. This requirement forms part of the very essence of the messianic message, and constitutes the heart of the Gospel ethos. The Teacher expresses this both through the medium of the commandment which He describes as "the greatest" (Matthew 22:38), and also in the form of a blessing, when in the Sermon on the Mount He proclaims: "Blessed are the merciful, for they shall obtain mercy" (Matthew 5:7).[6]

The Logic of Forgiveness

If one looks past the paradox of forgiveness and considers it strictly as a formula for salvation, there are four possible fates of a perpetrator and his victim. For the sake of clarity, let's imagine that a man named Joseph smashed a work of art of another man, Peter. The reason why is unimportant. Let's assume it was a personal treasure into which Peter had poured much of himself.

Joseph's destruction of Peter's property constitutes a sin that Peter must forgive. For the sake of his own salvation, Joseph must repent and try to make amends. The faith of each man obliges him to do the right thing, and if neither does what is required of him, then each risks his salvation.

Imagine, though, that Peter forgives Joseph's transgression, despite the lack of an apology or even an acknowledgment by Joseph of his destructive act. Peter has lived up to his creed and set himself right with God.

On the other hand, imagine that Peter cannot get over his loss or bring himself to forgive Joseph. Perhaps Joseph even apologizes and tries to offer Peter money or tickets to an expensive opera that he knows is one of Peter's favorites. In that case Joseph has set himself right with God, and Peter's salvation may be in jeopardy.

There is one last possibility: that Joseph apologizes and makes reparation to the best of his ability, and Peter forgives Joseph from his heart. In this case the two men are reconciled, and each is restored to communion with God.

This last scenario could come about in three possible ways: Peter's forgiveness could come first, and the graces won could help Joseph see his way to contrition; Joseph's remorse could come first, and his efforts to reconcile might help Peter do the difficult work of forgiving the loss of his cherished work; or forgiveness and remorse could happen simultaneously, in which case the reunion is God's own gift received in sincerity by two men who regret an unfortunate act.

Interestingly, although the "unfortunate act" involves anguish and a degradation of the one who behaved badly, it can become the bond of a deeper relationship if the men move forward prayerfully. As Scripture tells us, "In everything God works for good with those who love him" (Romans 8:28), and this case can show us how.

The opposite of love is not hatred but indifference. No matter what the relationship between Joseph and Peter was previous to this event, it's impossible for them to be indifferent toward one another afterward. The greatest animosity can be turned to love through the crucible of suffering. If these men come to pray for each other and for the gift of reconciliation, they will be bound by that action. They will mark each other's souls, so to speak, and their pilgrimages will become entangled—even against their wills.

Tokens of Value

In every sin there is something lost. Sometimes it's an object as easily defined as a painting, although as clear as such an object might seem, it's impossible to weigh the sentimental attachment and associations it may carry for its owner. Sometimes the sin is a betrayal of trust or a fit of temper that results in hurt feelings. It takes grace to get past what is lost.

Grace may seem to be beyond our grasp when we move from trifles to tragedies, but it is not. We are speaking of injuries among persons created in God's likeness, whom we love and who love us. These persons are the treasures of God's own heart. If our cherished relationships reflect Trinitarian love, we will see that perfect love become manifest in extraordinary ways.

In fact, as we wade through our sorrow, we may come to a purification that allows us to see that God is "all in all." Our faith teaches us that the essence of our being and our relationships can be restored in ways unimagined before we met God.

Calling to mind the sobering story in which Abraham is asked to sacrifice that which was dearest to him, his own beloved son, Isaac (see Genesis 22), we understand that in letting go and making an oblation of our treasures, we receive them back either literally or in a more perfect form. God doesn't will the destruction of anything that is good but has generously offered to restore all if we will but hand it over to him. This is at the heart of forgiveness, which is a letting go of what we love— even what was ripped from us through injustice. It isn't easy, but neither was Christ's road to Calvary, and that was the path to Easter and the reconciliation it offers.

God is our end, and ultimately his tokens of love are meant to bring us to him—either by our holding on to them with the correct spirit of detachment or by our losing them as oblations to his mercy. Ironically, it is the very love they bear—although making the suffering more intense—that has the capacity to transform us and restore the threefold image. And that is what will transpire for our own benefit.

...Forgiveness...bears witness that, in our world, love is stronger than sin. The martyrs of yesterday and today bear this witness to Jesus. Forgiveness is the fundamental condition of the reconciliation of the children of God with their Father and of men with one another. (CCC, 2844; see 2 Corinthians 5:18–21; *Dives in Misericordia*, 14)

It is essential that we never lose sight of the sin at the heart of injuries or diminish grave evils through excuses or disordered values. The Christian response to real harm is forgiveness; the greater harm is the breach of communion that will ensue if forgiveness is missing. We may never understand from this side of the veil, but our instructions are clear. We trust that the path of forgiveness bears within it the graces to make gifts and their loss the means to the deepest communion—an eternal communion with the Trinity.

CHAPTER THREE

The Altar of Love

The Bible is filled with examples of forgiveness, beginning with God himself, who had established a spousal covenant with the Jewish people. "I...will be your God, and you shall be my people," he told Moses (Leviticus 26:12), yet despite his constant love, his steadfast generosity, and the abundant miracles attesting to his fidelity, the nation of Israel repeatedly spurned the covenant by their sins. God sent numerous prophets to warn them of the disastrous consequences they were risking, but they often refused to listen. While the larger saga included the nation as a whole, God's mercy was offered on different levels, "social and communal, as well as individual and interior."[7]

The Temple Grounded in Mercy

After wandering in the desert for forty years, the Israelites emerged with the tablets of stone on which the Ten Commandments—given by God to Moses—were etched. These tablets were held in the ark, which awaited a permanent home in the temple, the construction of which would come centuries later when the Jewish monarchy was secured. Fully aware of both the nature of God and the inconstant hearts of the people, Solomon would dedicate the temple with a prayer that included the following:

...Then hear in heaven, and act, and judge your servants, condemning the guilty by bringing his conduct upon his own head, and vindicating the righteous by rewarding him according to his righteousness....

Let your eyes be open to the supplication of your servant, and to the supplication of your people Israel, giving ear to them whenever they call to you. For you separated them from among all the peoples of the earth, to be your heritage, and you declared through Moses, your servant, when you brought our fathers out of Egypt, O Lord GOD. (1 Kings 8:32, 52–53)

Solomon recognized that famine, pestilence, drought, defeat in battle, and exile were just punishments for Israel's waywardness, but he knew that contrition and prayer could bring a return of God's consolation and healing. In fact, the entire Old Testament is the unfolding of the breadth of God's constant love for his chosen people, who oscillated between gratitude and indifference in the face of his abiding mercy.

The Old Testament encourages people suffering from misfortune, especially those weighed down by sin—as also the whole of Israel, which had entered into the covenant with God—to appeal for mercy, and enables them to count upon it: it reminds them of His mercy in times of failure and loss of trust. Subsequently, the Old Testament gives thanks and glory for mercy every time that mercy is made manifest in the life of the people or in the lives of individuals.[8]

As we move into New Testament examples of forgiveness, we find the woman at the well conversing with Jesus, who responded to her skepticism, "If you knew the gift of God..." (John 4:10). Interestingly, her conversation with Our Lord also touched on the temple and where the faithful should worship God. Hers was a startling encounter with the one who told her everything she had done (see John 4:29). We can only assume that she subsequently turned from sin and began living her faith more carefully.

Orienting Our Own Temple

Christ's parables, discourses, conversations, and miracles offer myriad insights into the nature of God's mercy and encourage us to adopt the same generous attitude with others. One of the parables most illustrative of the many facets of the forgiveness of God is that of the prodigal son.

We recognize that the father in the story is a rich icon of our loving Creator. Both sons provide important lessons, of course, but for our purposes, I would like to turn to the elder brother. This is the one who hadn't strayed from his father's house and who hadn't squandered his inheritance through bad behavior. If we've been personally injured by the bad behavior of others and are contemplating the necessary response, we would do well to meditate on what happened after the prodigal returned and received the embrace of his father.

> Now his elder son was in the field; and as he came and drew near to the house, he heard music and dancing. And he called one of the servants and asked what this meant. And he said to him, "Your brother has come, and your father has killed the fatted calf, because he has received him safe and sound." But he was angry and refused to go in. His father came out and entreated him,

17

but he answered his father, "Behold, these many years I have served you, and I never disobeyed your command; yet you never gave me a kid, that I might make merry with my friends. But when this son of yours came, who has devoured your living with harlots, you killed for him the fatted calf!" And he said to him, "Son, you are always with me, and all that is mine is yours. It was fitting to make merry and be glad, for this your brother was dead, and is alive; he was lost, and is found." (Luke 15:25–32)

For all the grief suffered over the corruption of his younger son, the father's distress didn't end when the long-anticipated reunion finally took place. His subsequent suffering was caused by the lack of communion between his two sons. When it appears that we have a claim to the moral high ground, yet the forgiveness we count on for our "minor" sins is also extended for the gravest of errors, it is entirely possible for us to become angry—especially when the other's sins have harmed us.

Not only will those who have hurt us find God's mercy if they repent, but God expects us to forgive them as well. While this story, and Christ's admonition to forgive "seventy times seven times," might lead one to believe that we can legitimately withhold forgiveness until the perpetrator shows remorse, later chapters will show that is a dangerous proposition. For now let us keep before our eyes the movement of the father toward his prodigal son "while he was yet at a distance" (Luke 15:20). If we are friends with God and try to remain in his grace, we should be able to do likewise, and he will help us. In fact, his own action within us will bring about the reconciliation, if we allow it.

Mary as an Icon of the Perfect Temple

As noted in the previous chapter, the greatest biblical example we have, apart from God himself, is the Blessed Mother. She understood well that salvation history is a series of illustrations of God's loving overtures to sinful man. Although her Immaculate Conception is not explicit in Scripture, it provides one more glimpse into the nature of God's mercy: He reached down and preserved her from sin so that, "when the time had fully come" (Galatians 4:4), she could respond in total freedom to his proposal.

From that auspicious beginning we find a perfect progression to the Annunciation, where the angel Gabriel invited Our Lady to be the mother of the Messiah. Knowing that both her own conception and this invitation were unmerited gifts from God, she embraced the most immediate means she had of sharing them with another. She went "with haste" to visit her cousin Elizabeth, who greeted her in joy. Mary included mercy—that marvelous dimension of the truth about God—in her *Magnificat*:

> My soul magnifies the Lord …
> for he has regarded the low estate of his handmaiden.
> For behold, henceforth all generations will call me
> blessed;
> for he who is mighty has done great things for me,
> and holy is his name.
> And his mercy is on those who fear him
> from generation to generation.
>
> …
>
> He has put down the mighty from their thrones,
> and exalted those of low degree;

...
He has helped his servant Israel,
in remembrance of his mercy. (Luke 1:46b, 48–50, 52, 54)

In her humility Mary knew of her unworthiness, and thus she referred all that is good back to God, its source. The same should be true in our efforts to live righteously. Our good actions, as paltry as they are, only serve as the tiniest reflections of his surpassing kindness. As St. Paul noted, "God is at work in you, both to will and to work for his good pleasure" (Philippians 2:13). When we do as we ought, it is actually God—the source of all good—working through us, and we are thus tied to the divine love that cannot help but forgive.

Our Lady's generous visit to her cousin was only the beginning of her oblation of gratitude to God, as John Paul II noted in *Dives in Misericordia*:

> Mary is also the one who obtained mercy in a particular
> and exceptional way, as no other person has. At the same
> time, still in an exceptional way, she made possible with
> the sacrifice of her heart her own sharing in revealing
> God's mercy.... No one has received into his heart, as
> much as Mary did, that mystery, that truly divine dimen-
> sion of the redemption effected on Calvary by means of
> the death of the Son, together with the sacrifice of her
> maternal heart, together with her definitive "fiat."[9]

As quiet as Mary may be in the pages of Holy Scripture, we must recognize that our salvation is grounded in her sacrifice. God's offer of reconciliation found its home in a heart that would live that forbearance heroically. Her very body was offered as the bridge of reconciliation, giving flesh to the Lamb of God.

Although Mary's heart was shredded by the obstinacy of many around her—who would try to stone her son, repeatedly mock him and reject him, and ultimately torture and kill him— she stood by not in stoic detachment but with her heart fully engaged and open to all. Knowing that God's mercy had invited her into this communion, she was not going to hold back from it nor shrink from the suffering it entailed. For that we are deeply grateful.

The Promises of Pentecost

After Our Lord's resurrection, through which the world was reconciled to God, the Holy Spirit was poured out upon the apostles at Pentecost. Peter stood up and spoke, referencing the book of Joel:

> And I will show wonders in the heaven above
> and signs on the earth beneath,
> blood, and fire, and vapor of smoke;
> the sun shall be turned into darkness
> and the moon into blood,
> before the day of the Lord comes,
> the great and manifest day.
> And it shall be that whoever calls on the name of the
> Lord shall be saved. (Acts 2:19–21)

While we might look longingly for tongues of fire or the physical phenomena that Peter outlines, which easily pass for material wonders, it is essential that we don't miss the quieter miracles in our midst—those that have to do with the healing of hearts and conversion to God. Those of us, especially, who are crushed by pain or crippled by incidents beyond our understanding should know how the shades of darkness compare to the light of Christ. What is a material flood compared to the rush of healing at the hands of the Holy Spirit? And how could one not relate the effects of an earthquake to the crumbling of our prisons upon being released from the shackles of resentment?

These are miracles that come from forgiveness, that flow when God's mercy is fully mirrored in our lives. These are the miracles that matter, because they will last throughout eternity, when the sun and moon are no more. This is what the Holy Spirit intimated to those astonished listeners who wondered if Peter and his companions were drunk (see Acts 2:13).

The people of God moved from the desert to the temple, and now they move from the temple to the holy altar where Christ laid down his life to teach us the extent of his mercy. The Mystical Body has been brought to the New Jerusalem, of which the Virgin—Our Lady of Mercy—is the model. The pilgrimage of every disciple must follow the same pattern, so that each person is grounded in that same Spirit and truth.

Jesus, in whom we are reborn, told his disciples, "Destroy this temple, and in three days I will raise it up" (John 2:19), and so it came to pass. The injuries over which we grieve were party to that destruction, and his rising proves that mercy is greater than those injuries are. Jesus says, "Behold, I make all things new" (Revelation 21:5). Trust him, for your broken heart is precisely what he came to heal.

CHAPTER FOUR

Nuts and Bolts

As foundational as forgiveness is to our Christian faith, the actual process is remarkably murky to those who contemplate its practical application. From a distance it can look like a dismissive action—excusing both the gravity of the wrong that has been done and the corresponding pain in the victim. It can look like an endorsement of injustice, especially if it leads to the perpetrator going unpunished. It may also look like a setup for being a doormat, by which one is robbed of his bodily integrity, his possessions, and ultimately his dignity. Is that really what God asks of us?

In this chapter we will look at the practical steps to forgiving an injury. The rest of the book will reveal the answers to the questions about what happens next.

Forgiving All Injuries

The first question to ask is, Who is to receive your forgiveness? The answer is absolutely everyone who has harmed you in any way. Whether you think that the injuries are too massive to contemplate or too small to warrant your attention, everything is included in Our Lord's admonition.

Matthew's Gospel offers the account of a servant whose enormous debt the king forgave and yet who subsequently refused to forgive a pittance owed him by a fellow servant (see Matthew 18:21–35). The parable is instructive because it relates to both seeking forgiveness and forgiving. We learn that any sin committed here on earth pales in comparison to how we offend God, but we also see that the smallest of debts needs to be dealt with. Sins cannot simply be ignored but must be forgiven; the slate must be wiped clean.

It might be easier to start with small incidents, for they carry less pain and are often more isolated than the big issues. Take, for instance, the uncomplicated occasion of planning to meet a friend for coffee—a friend who unfortunately forgot the appointment. You might have cleared your schedule for the morning and waited a long time for her, assuming that she was caught in traffic. She didn't show, she didn't call, and she didn't apologize. You're understandably upset.

Let's imagine that your friend remembered the oversight the next day and called, but she didn't seem to attach the same weight to her mistake as you did. Her apology sounded trivial compared to how you felt about the slight. Your anger grows— as much due to her seeming indifference as because of her initial neglect.

The sooner this is forgiven the better, but what does that entail? An act of the will. You must say to yourself, "I forgive my friend for her mistake."

The forgiveness is not an excuse for the slight. Objectively, the friend was uncharitable, even after remembering the missed rendezvous. There is no excuse. The act of forgiveness is your decision to bear this injury and to let it go, not to diminish it in hopes that it will dissolve on its own. It needs to be dealt with forthrightly, for it is just such injuries that make up much of our lives as we hobble through this fallen world.

It's entirely true that friends take up our time, neglect important things, and can be self-absorbed and obtuse when it comes to our feelings. The very same goes for us, no matter how we may pride ourselves on our generosity. The only response to others is love. St. Paul is firm in reminding us that love "bears all things, believes all things, hopes all things, endures all things" (1 Corinthians 13:7).

Following the firm act of forgiveness for the objective wrong in the matter, you could take your anger to prayer. If you weren't so conscious of the value of your time, perhaps you would have been less angry. Perhaps you could have looked about you calmly as you waited and prayed for the people you saw. Did you stop to consider that what she was doing may have been so important that a coffee date seemed insignificant? Is it possible that she couldn't tell you about a larger crisis that put your plans out of her mind? Is it possible that you take yourself a little too seriously at times?

All of these thoughts will be clearer after the act of forgiveness, as will the firm intention to bring a book next time in case you are caught waiting again. A few more episodes with this dear soul may allow you to categorize her as beloved but unreliable, and to rethink such plans. Some people will ever be thus. Changing your expectations can prevent you from the same injury later.

But that is not the primary point. We harm others and are harmed in return. It is important not to let those defects—especially the ones we're so careful to avoid—cause us to become angry or prideful. Any virtues we exhibit are God's grace, not cause to lord it over others.

What About the Apology?

Many people nurse injuries and harbor resentments and pain, withholding forgiveness until the culprit expresses sorrow. This is a dangerous way to proceed for two important reasons.

First, if your forgiveness hinges on the other's contrition, then he or she is exercising a control over you that is entirely unwarranted. If you put forgiveness in the hands of the wrongdoer, then you hand your eternal destiny to a finite creature—and one who has already shown a disdain for your dignity. Although you are the victim of whatever harm the person displayed, the requirements you have established hold your soul hostage.

Furthermore, what sort of apology will satisfy you? Sincerity is almost impossible to gauge. If an apology is breezy or dismissive, such as that of the woman who missed her coffee date, you may be angrier after the apology than before. And some apologies are more insulting than the behavior they're meant to excuse. Thus, to pin our forgiveness on the contrition of others is very difficult and sometimes only confuses the issue.

The second problem with such a criterion is that you may never see the person again. In the case of a hit-and-run driver, a large part of the offense is the cowardly nature of the one who will not return and acknowledge the deed. Especially in the realm of childhood injuries, it is often a fact that by the time you're ready to embark on naming the injury and forgiving it, the wrongdoer has died. In other settings—such as terrorism, war, and criminal activities—there may never be a particular face attached to the harm inflicted. Yet these injuries too, in time, must be forgiven.

While the heartfelt contrition of the other certainly might help us forgive, we cannot afford to stand on ceremony in this critical work. (Of course, we're obliged to offer our own apologies whenever possible, to help others forgive our trespasses against them.) It's good to meditate on the example of St. Stephen. He forgave the men who stoned him while they were still in the act! Not only was there no contrition on their part, but there was no relenting in their depraved deed. Stephen's urgency to forgive was obvious, for he was on his way to meet God (see Acts 7:54–60).

We may not have the privilege of knowing the hour of our death. Rather than thinking about what another should do on our behalf, let's forgive all injuries. The limitations of others must not cripple us or keep us from doing what God firmly commands. Even if an injustice has held us bound for some time, God wants us to be free.

Probing the Wound

Sometimes an injury comes from a specific event, like the neglected coffee date described above. Other times wounds accumulate over a matter of years (as examples in the following chapters will illustrate). In many instances we are so close to a harmful situation that we cannot actually see what happened. In such cases it can be helpful to confide in another person.

The process of choosing this person should be made easier through prayer and discernment. It must be someone who will hold all the information entrusted to him or her in the strictest confidence. It must be someone who can be a boulder of strength to us during the venting process. The person may know the parties in question or not; perhaps we will choose a professional counselor. What is important is that the person have a firm working knowledge of the appropriate boundaries in everyday life.[10]

When the victim is ready and comfortable, together they may begin to carefully unpack what has transpired.[11] The confidant's primary job is to listen. This listening requires an ability to interpret what is said and what is not said. The feedback at first is simply to extract the necessary information to assess the situation. What may be immediately remarkable to the counselor is the comfort that the wounded person has with some shocking events and the lack of discernment about what actions actually crossed a line.

Years ago, one such conversation between friends gave rise to accounts of emotional abuse that the listener found appalling, and yet the victim didn't see those elements as part of the problem. She was in the process of outlining other troubling factors in her life and had to gently be drawn back to the initial landscape that she had assumed was normal, to see that the roots of the problem were more complex than she had initially assumed. The sensitivities of the listener are paramount. Even if she doesn't have a degree in counseling or psychology, if she is in a state of grace and understands the normal give-and-take of family life, her instincts will guide her through these exchanges.

Occasionally the friend may have to point out the gravity of a wound. The wounded person may have built up defenses or walled off areas to hide from a sense of shame. We tend to accommodate buried memories in such a way that they rise to the surface in a detached form—so much so that the friend may not believe that we're describing ourselves. She may weep as we sit there numb, having lost that part of our soul long ago. The body has all sorts of coping mechanisms that work extremely well in helping us survive, but working them backwards—like unrolling a ball of twine—can be a maddening, complicated process.

An initial response to such help may be one of grief, especially if the corruption of a child is involved. When the Holy Spirit guides such a conversation, he will take us into the Garden of Gethsemane first. There we may weep with Our Lord over the sin in the world, the inability of goodness to prevail, and the suffering that the world must endure until it can find its way to God. We mourn our own lost innocence, the depravity of some souls, and the chain of events that culminated in the harmful situation. It is on this journey of sorrow and discovery that the spiritual maternity of the friend is most needed, as she draws forth the beauty of the child of God who was harmed. It is in her eyes that the victim can rediscover her own dignity and value. Tears that may have been repressed for decades must fall before the healing can take place—just as an infected wound must expel life-threatening toxins that would undermine a full recovery.

Eventually the injury will be broken down and analyzed. We should examine the various dimensions of it, especially when several persons are complicit in the situation. In such a case each will have to be forgiven for his or her part in the injury.

We may want to make excuses for the behavior of others. Hopefully our friend will be firm in reminding us that sins are sins. Extenuating circumstances can be studied later within the light of the grace attached to forgiving.

It is entirely possible that with a fresh set of eyes on an age-old wound, there will be new insights and a stunning new encounter with anger—even rage. It may be frightening to see family members in a new light, especially those with whom one has interacted over the years. That light might preclude the casual breeziness that has become routine in a relationship. There may be a terror in acknowledging the harms, for they may undermine our ability to carry on as we have for years.

If the revelations are too much, perhaps we can put the process away for a time. But note that anger in itself is not a sin. It can be a righteous response to an injustice, an entirely justifiable reaction that we would have on behalf of anyone else being harmed. Often we cannot see the facts clearly when it is our own story.

That is why the friend's input and perspective are so important. There may be resistance on the part of the injured person, in which case the process will take time—and more than likely, prayer and sacrifice. The gift of friendship comes with serious responsibilities, and this is one of them. I sometimes tremble at the thought of what God entrusts to me.

Expressing Forgiveness

Next comes the act of forgiveness, which we can make in the presence of our friend or on our own. Some may prefer to say these words before the Blessed Sacrament. The important thing is that we say them with firmness, when the wound is understood and the grief has been vented. If it is done prematurely, more bitterness may arise later. But even that is not an insurmountable problem. We can simply extend the process and forgive again.

There are two dimensions to the expression of forgiveness that need to be explored. The first concerns emotions surrounding forgiveness. In all honesty, many people simply don't feel like forgiving. Even though it's possible that we've been deadened in certain ways due to overwhelming pain, we do live in a culture overly absorbed in feelings. In many instances sentiment has replaced orderly thought. Instead of catechizing ourselves on vice and virtue, the boundaries of religion, or the principles of reason, we cling to our feelings and prefer to listen to our gut. Sometimes, with a well-formed conscience, that gut will guide us well, but in some matters—especially when we've suffered trauma—emotion shouldn't lead our responses.

Forgiveness is a decision, not a feeling. We begin with God's command, we go through a grieving process if necessary, and when the time is right, we make an act of forgiveness. It is as simple as saying, "I forgive." As with penance after confession, a goodwill gesture is a way of expressing the sincerity of our words, and it would be good to pray for the person or his intentions. Feelings may follow, but they are not necessarily signposts concerning what we have done.

If feelings of resentment or bitterness rise after the first act of forgiveness, then make another. In chapter twelve we will see that the forgiveness process can be incremental in many cases, requiring a repeated process. Don't be aggravated or impatient, for as long as you're moving forward, you're healing. Some things take time, and it is time well spent.

The second issue that concerns many is wondering if they are required to confront the one who has harmed them, expressing their act of forgiveness. Ultimately this is not necessary. In faith we know the power of prayer, and our sincere prayers for the other's well-being are enough. If we are genuinely praying that the person find and remain in a state of grace, we will meet him or her in heaven. If we can contemplate that reunion without anxiety or bitterness, then that is an excellent indication that we are moving past the wounds.

31

Ultimately the decision about expressing forgiveness is a matter of prayer. The other person may be ashamed to bring the matter up. Perhaps he or she apologized in the past before we were ready to forgive. In this situation a letter expressing the fact that we have let go of the injury might be a real consolation to the other. The letter could bolster the person's faith that his or her prayers and contrition were of worth. We might truly be surprised at how things have changed if years have passed.

The last step in the process includes the sacrament of penance, which is necessary if there has been any resentment or bitterness toward those who inflicted injury. As natural as such a response is, it must be confessed for the harm it did to the soul. The essential element is to state to the priest that you have borne resentment against a particular person for a particular length of time. Explaining why is beyond the realm of the sacrament and can cause you either to relive the injury or to make excuses. The latter, especially, can be distracting for the priest, who must be attentive to your sin, not the sin of the one who injured you.

Apart from the question of mental illness and the various pathologies that flow from deep trauma, this straightforward approach to forgiveness should be sufficient to reap the rewards of reconciliation. The following chapters show how different women have benefitted by the process and what graces are available to those who have the courage to take God's commands to heart—for he is a merciful Father who wants the very best for his beloved daughters.

CHAPTER FIVE

Repairing the Sanctuary

While the fourth commandment, "Honor your father and mother," is entirely clear about the debt we owe our parents, that obligation gets very complicated when there are troubling dysfunctions at the heart of family life. Of course, no family is perfect, and living in close quarters with a handful of fallen souls (while clinging to our own defects and failures) causes everyone to stagger unevenly along the path to eternity. Even so, there are some breaches of charity that are so heinous as to virtually blind the young to the paternal love of a Father-God and the maternal care of Holy Mother Church. For these the standard calls to forgiveness must be carefully couched in the language of patient love.

Trust Betrayed

Jill was raised in a comfortable suburb, with a father and mother, a picket fence, and a dog. Her only brother was a soft-spoken boy seven years older than herself whom she adored. Often left to wander the house on their own, curiosity eventually led them to their parents' bedroom, where they discovered a large stash of pornography hidden by one side of the bed. Jill didn't understand her brother's interest in the magazines, but if he found them worthwhile, she would remain by him.

She flipped from page to page, avidly reading the abundant cartoons, trying to grasp the unfamiliar genre of humor. That the women in the drawings were busty and naked only mildly shocked her. It was the curious punch lines and the bizarre settings that mystified her. Who were these people?

Evidently Jill's brother didn't limit himself to perusing the lame jokes. Whatever he found in those pages piqued his curiosity and led him to try things with his sister that she didn't understand. His unfortunate response became routine.

Jill only knew that she loved her brother. She didn't like his physical experimentation and yet intuited that she must never speak of it. Her relationships with her mother and father became less forthright, for as she reasoned, they ultimately must be a party to the magazines that led to her great discomfort. She was alone, and there was no objective reason she could name for her isolation, other than a deep, deep revulsion at what was happening.

Since those pre-Internet years, when smut was wrapped in brown paper and hidden under mattresses, the pornography industry has exploded—on websites, in magazines, and in films. This so-called victimless dimension of the modern world actually has millions of victims—from the women (and children!) objectified in the images to those who suffer at the hands of the porn addicts who act upon them. Just because it is widespread and more mainstream today doesn't remove the grievous harms that pornography inflicts on all it touches.

What makes pornography in the home so egregious is that the family is supposed to provide a sanctuary for those within its precincts, so that children can safely learn about God, the truths of the faith, and the challenges of the wider world. The dynamic that is supposed to exist within the home is outlined in John Paul II's letter *Familiaris Consortio* (The Family in the Modern World):

> A fundamental opportunity for building such a commu-
> nion is constituted by the educational exchange between
> parents and children, in which each gives and receives.
> By means of love, respect and obedience towards their
> parents, children offer their specific and irreplaceable
> contribution to the construction of an authentically
> human and Christian family. They will be aided in this
> if parents exercise their unrenounceable authority as a
> true and proper "ministry," that is, as a service to the
> human and Christian well-being of their children, and
> in particular as a service aimed at helping them acquire
> a truly responsible freedom, and if parents maintain a
> living awareness of the "gift" they continually receive
> from their children.[12]

A glance around us today clearly shows that there is something terribly wrong with the family. It not only neglects its duties to strengthen the faith of its members but often welcomes the very evils that it is charged with defending against. From question-able song lyrics to vulgar sit-coms, from broken vows to neglect of catechesis, children are left prey to myriad harms that under-mine their purity and ability to trust in the adults around them.

There are several legitimate questions that flow from such circumstances. How does a grown person regain the trust that was lost at a tender age? How does one express filial piety when the parents were negligent? What obligations remain when a woman realizes that her family forms a toxic environment?

Helen was raised a Catholic, even though her parents' marriage broke down amidst alcohol-related acrimony. She and her siblings were all quite young when they fled with their mother. They found themselves slipping further and further into poverty, until Stan came along with an offer to provide for them all. Helen's mother welcomed the opportunity for her children to find some stability, and yet food, shelter, and clothing came at a very high price.

Stan had a violent temper and very little patience. Forced to call him "Dad," the children were cowed into silence whenever he was at home and beaten for the smallest infractions of his rules. Equally painful was his abuse of their mother, which added to their fear and confusion. God the Father even became a terrifying figure, for every thought of paternal attention was colored by stern bullying.

It was the birth of Helen's first child that led her to understand that she had to forgive her mother. A trusted friend offered her the valuable advice, "Don't bring that poison into your own situation." As Helen prayed she realized that she couldn't blame her mother, who had simply felt that she had no other options. Her mother had been trapped in her dilemma.

There were others Helen had difficulty forgiving. Although there were always signs of child abuse in the family, no one at her Catholic school ever stepped in or asked any questions. Many cries for help went unheeded. Those resentments also had to be dealt with.

Helen's healing came through praying the rosary. In that prayer—after many tears and pleas—she was given the grace she asked for. There was an overnight transformation, and she awoke basking in the love of God. Only one whose image of fatherhood was so sullied could understand the deep conversion she experienced. The gaping hole in her heart—a hole lined with a shrinking fear—was now filled with a deep affection for God the Father.

To this day there are no intermediaries who model that paternal love for Helen, for her own marriage broke down after the birth of her three children. Thus her healing was entirely supernatural. She understood that God's message to her was "I'm all you need," and indeed, he alone has been sufficient.

Insidious Harms

The difficulty with family dysfunction is that not all injuries are so stark. Although Jill was quick to sense that chastity is preferred to impropriety, the corrosion that resulted from being objectified at such a young age was harder to address. While Helen's bruises were visible, her crushed sense of fatherly love was less obvious. In both cases the sanctuary had been grievously violated: The men who should have safeguarded those entrusted to their care were entirely negligent. Sadly, their shortcomings within the family circle undermined their children's ability to create healthy relationships in the future. Furthermore, the mothers and teachers who stood nearby enabled the abuse, whether through fear or their own neglect.

So what is our responsibility amidst this chaos of sin? As icons of Holy Mother Church, we are called to be bridges of reconciliation between fathers and their children, between God and all of creation. This is impossible if we are unhealed ourselves and if we retain any bitterness toward fatherhood or God. Although we can never excuse the men who sully the name of father, we must forgive them for the sake of all whose salvation depends on their ability to trust God.

In *Familiaris Consortio* John Paul II reminds us of how much families depend on reconciliation for their well-being:

> Family communion can only be preserved and perfected through a great spirit of sacrifice. It requires, in fact, a ready and generous openness of each and all to understanding, to forbearance, to pardon, to reconciliation. There is no family that does not know how selfishness, discord, tension and conflict violently attack and at times mortally wound its own communion: hence there arise the many and varied forms of division in family life. But, at the same time, every family is called by the God of peace to have the joyous and renewing experience of "reconciliation," that is, communion reestablished, unity restored. In particular, participation in the sacrament of Reconciliation and in the banquet of the one Body of Christ offers to the Christian family the grace and the responsibility of overcoming every division and of moving towards the fullness of communion willed by God, responding in this way to the ardent desire of the Lord: "that they may be one."[13]

We must follow Helen's example and beg for the grace to forgive. Perhaps we will receive it overnight as she did, or perhaps we will not feel the love of God so immediately. Regardless, we must step out in confidence, knowing that forgiveness is the right thing to pursue and that we and our loved ones will benefit by it.

Communion between God and his creation came with the shedding of Christ's precious blood; communion in our families can begin with the shedding of our deeply held resentments. Whether or not fathers' hearts are turned to their children may hinge on the prayers we offer on their behalf. Let's do our part.

Seeking Peace Amidst Trials

Those involved in twelve-step programs will be familiar with at least the opening lines of the "Serenity Prayer," which is entirely Christian in its outlook:

> God, grant me the serenity to accept the things I cannot
>   change;
> the courage to change the things I can;
> and the wisdom to know the difference.
> Living one day at a time; enjoying one moment at a time;
> accepting hardships as the pathway to peace;
> taking, as he did, this sinful world as it is, not as I would
>   have it;
> trusting that he will make all things right if I surrender
>   to his will;
> that I may be reasonably happy in this life
> and supremely happy with him forever in the next.
> Amen.[14]

The key to serenity is assessing what can be changed and what must rest as it is in our lives. It is essential that we take a prayerful look at the landscape within our families. Granted, conversion is possible—and greatly to be desired—for everyone in our lives, but until that happens, sin will take its course. Those hardened by sin will be unkind to those around them; those habituated to particular sins will spread their effects. Our work at reconciliation cannot ignore these realities, but it can inject the gentle truths and healing overtures that create lifelines for those looking for change.

This is the wisdom that the saints brought to their families, and this is the grace that allows the victims of yesterday to be apostles of forgiveness today. Surrendering to Our Lord's commandment to forgive doesn't abase us but elevates us above the chaos in our lives, so that—with lamps held high—we can show those still suffering a path to peace. Thus Helen kept the poison of bitterness away from her children, and she modeled for them a healthy way to live in this fallen world.

John Paul II was fond of repeating, "Families, become what you are!"[15] His love for family life was always close to his heart, and he defined its mission in his writing:

> The essence and role of the family are in the final analysis specified by love. Hence the family has the mission to guard, reveal and communicate love, and this is a living reflection of and a real sharing in God's love for humanity and the love of Christ the Lord for the Church his bride.[16]

It is essential that we not be bound by corrupt versions of family life that sought to crush us before we could discover the Holy Family. Remember Our Lord's dire warning about scandalizing the little ones (see Matthew 18:6–6). We can find solace through the example and intercession of St. Joseph, who stood guard over the pure souls in his care. Surely he will join in the prayers of those whose earthly fathers betrayed them. Turn to that "just man," the patron of the universal Church, for as surely as he protects that bride, he will lead you in paths of healing and strength. And God will "restore to you the years which the swarming locust has eaten" (Joel 2:25).

CHAPTER SIX

Remothering Through Mary

When family life is more a cradle of pain than a source of consolation and growth, the path to forgiveness may be long. The pathologies of a dysfunctional home are often so insidious that it can take years to isolate them and see them for what they truly are.

When a woman has been deprived of healthy maternal affection in particular, the wound cuts to the core of her person. The Blessed Mother stands ready to console such hearts. She, the Seat of Wisdom, is entirely aware that reaching out for help may be difficult for those whose filial trust was betrayed early in life.

The Long Forgiveness

Leah's path to forgiveness was just such a journey, since her wounds had accumulated over many years. Her parents were nominally Protestant, but instead of faith the priority was social prestige and the outward conformity necessary to attain it. Her mother had married a man she dearly loved—a man who was, at heart, benevolent and scholarly. Yet his alcoholism worked to destroy the family in subtle ways. Her mother's subsequent frustration was exacerbated by her deep disappointment in Leah, who was not the blonde, lithe daughter she had hoped for. She criticized Leah at length. Leah's three brothers took their cues from their mother, combining insults of their own with discreet physical attacks.

The family culture was shallow to nonexistent; the parents often travelled, and even when they were home there were no family meals. Cocktail hour each evening was sacrosanct. The feeble kindliness of Leah's father did little to protect her from abuse, for his gentle character was overshadowed by drink and the stronger personality of his wife. Leah grew to hate all the members of her family for the constant mockery and painful rejection.

She had some solace in the succession of gentle black women who were hired to care for her over the years—women who sang spirituals and called on the name of Jesus all day long, whether tired or happy. And Leah enjoyed her time alone with books and nature. But as she grew into adolescence, the usual rebellion set in. There was plenty of money, which she spent freely on parties, cigarettes, and alcohol. These served to numb the deep emptiness in her soul.

Curiously, when Leah went away to college, she found herself surrounded in her dormitory by Catholics. Although these girls socialized at her same mad pace, Leah noted that they were quite happy and didn't drink to mask frustration or loneliness. They also went to confession regularly and never failed to get up for Mass on Sunday. Their contented faith was in concert with that of the caregivers Leah remembered so fondly from childhood.

Intrigued, Leah began to take instructions in the Catholic faith and attend Mass. That may have unleashed the series of providential choices that turned her life around. She began to take note of the deep sufferings of others, and she knew that she had to find a way to be happy. With whatever grace she had at the time—and it is clear that God was at work to begin the healing process—she chose love. That choice included letting go of bitterness and making healthier decisions in her everyday life.

Leah married well, started a family, and began attending ACOA meetings, the twelve-step program for adult children of alcoholics. There she discovered that she had been part of a classic alcoholic household, filled with resentment, favoritism, and emotional abuse. Later she discovered that the love of a good and patient man, the inherent lessons of motherhood, and the sacraments combined over the years to bring her to a measure of compassion for her parents' deep misery, which stemmed from their own horrid experiences in childhood.

At one point a wise Ugandan priest offered pivotal advice in confession as Leah bewailed her failure to forgive her mother. He asked if she was trying to take revenge, to which Leah gave a firm no—in fact she had tried unsuccessfully to repair the relationship. He said, "Then God will give forgiveness."

Leah answered that she didn't feel that forgiveness; she was unable to. Father reiterated in his calming voice, "Your feelings make no difference; God will give forgiveness in his time. You have made your confession; you are not trying to take revenge; you will be given forgiveness."

Just as we are unable to say, "Jesus is Lord," without the help of the Spirit (see 1 Corinthians 12:3), all good things originate in him. Sin undermines the dignity of the souls of both the injured and the injuring parties, and God offers his own pardon as well as the grace to pardon others. "Through him, with him, and in him": This exchange manifests our response to the privileged invitation to participate in the divine life of God; this is the beauty of our incarnational faith, a beauty that we hardly recognize until the raging waters of this world threaten to overcome us. God provides—even the words of forgiveness that will emanate from our lips.

Leah discovered that the priest was absolutely right. The grace of forgiveness was a gift for which she needed to beg, and subsequently she did so. Time passed, and the mystery of forgiveness began to flower. Her mother changed little, remaining abusive and insulting well into her nineties. Regardless, Leah stays close to the sacraments, confessing her anger and resentment when necessary.

Leah has also learned to keep a healthy distance for the sake of protecting her own heart. Light notes and brief phone calls allow her to remain in touch with her mother without the inevitable sting that closer contact would entail. Thus she avoids the occasions of sin that her mother might offer. Leah prays and makes sacrifices for her mother, offers Masses for her conversion, and tells her that she is very much loved—which is entirely true.

The years of forgiveness have allowed Leah to turn the relationship around. Through the intercession of Mary, to whom Leah turned in order to receive the maternal love of which she had been deprived, a spiritual motherhood has blossomed in her own soul. It is a maternity that allows her to enfold her own bitter mother in a prayerful embrace that she hopes will straddle this world and the next.

Restoring the Image

Part of the truth revealed by the Incarnation is the importance of our corporeity—our having bodies. Although Christ stooped to walk among us, the greater import is that we were lifted into a fleshly union with him that will have no end. "The unity of soul and body is so profound that one has to consider the soul to be the 'form' of the body" (CCC, 365). To that end the Church encourages tactile and visual aids to our faith, such as statues and paintings. Indeed, part of the rich patrimony of the Church is that our churches are filled with tremendous pieces of art that help lift our hearts to God.

Unfortunately, for a series of complex reasons—both theological and political—a controversy over icons rocked the Eastern Church in the eighth and ninth centuries. Many were confused in thinking that venerating sacred images could lead to idolatry or superstition, and thus a wave of iconoclasm ensued, which destroyed a tremendous amount of religious art. Pope Gregory II's response was eloquent on the benefit of images as means of drawing closer to God. For indeed, when honored properly, images can provide priceless windows into eternity.

Images of Mary, in particular, augment Christian devotion, for they recall the integral part she played in salvation history. As powerful as the holy rosary is as a method of prayer, and as sure as Mary's place is in heaven as mediatrix of all graces, her images reveal a human dimension of her maternity—the beauty of her face.

One remarkable healing that bears on our topic is found in the autobiography of Thérèse of Lisieux, *Story of a Soul*. The beloved youngest child of an intensely pious family became bedridden at the age of nine due to a perplexing illness. She suffered grievously in both mind and body. At a dire point one of her anguished sisters stormed heaven, and these prayers were answered in a profound way. St. Thérèse, the Little Flower, recounts that a statue of Mary placed at the foot of her bed was the instrument of God's healing grace:

> Finding no help on earth, poor little Thérèse had also turned toward the Mother of heaven, and prayed with all her heart that she take pity on her. All of a sudden the Blessed Virgin appeared *beautiful* to me, so *beautiful* that never had I seen anything so attractive; her face was suffused with an ineffable benevolence and tenderness, but what penetrated to the very depths of my soul was the "*ravishing smile of the Blessed Virgin.*" At that instant, all my pain disappeared, and two large tears glistened on my eyelashes, and flowed down my cheek silently, but they were tears of unmixed joy.[17]

Thérèse's mother had died when she was an infant, and as much as her sisters and father doted on her, there was a particular wound awaiting a maternal touch. Mary indeed showed herself a loving mother in that moment.

While we cannot count on such miraculous encounters with Our Lady, pious devotions through her images can have a powerful effect, especially for those seeking to be healed of mother-wounds. Mary is your mother as well. She will be delighted to be invited into your heart.

Let Mary Heal You

Others have had similar, if more subtle, transformations through Our Lady's healing countenance, even those who were only introduced to her much later in life. Alice was a convert who had suffered through a long, difficult relationship with her mother—a mother she now realizes was suffering from mental illness during Alice's formative years. Her mother often repeated curious stories from Alice's childhood that made little sense, and she even berated Alice for being a difficult baby.

Well into adulthood, Alice noted that many of her relationships were stunted and that establishing trust was difficult. Although she was very smart, successful in school, and happily married, unexpected obstacles arose that she could not ignore.

A careful study of child psychology provided the critical information Alice needed to move forward. She began to connect her own collection of idiosyncrasies with a particular diagnosis: affect regulation disorder. She realized that key elements of a healthy maternal relationship were missing from her life—especially the mother's smile that an infant internalizes for its own well-being. Alice's mother had scowled and fretted throughout those years. Thus when Alice was alone or anxious, there was no comforting maternal image to draw upon for solace.

Constant acts of forgiveness, reliance on the sacraments, and a firm attempt to make the Blessed Mother an abiding companion brought about the healing that Alice desired. She consistently meditated upon a variety of Marian images, by which the maternal smile that she craved was restored in the gentle face of Christ's own mother. This is a true mother given to each of us from the very hand of God's Son! (see John 19:26–27).

Alice trusted firmly in the words of the prophet Joel, in which God assures his people that, after a drought, "the threshing floors shall be full of grain, the vats shall overflow with wine and oil" (Joel 2:24). Despite her tenuous start, Alice's heart has healed and expanded immeasurably, and she has subsequently nurtured other women through Bible studies, books, articles, and generous friendships. As a mother and grandmother, she has spread in a variety of venues the critical message of forgiveness—a message she would never have understood without her own deep pain. Her witness proves that our fidelity to the promises of God will bear fruit in remarkable forms. Like our mother Mary, we should allow our healed souls to magnify the Lord by loving—no matter the cost.

Thanks to the Church's continued encouragement of Christian art, we have thousands of Marian images at our disposal. These images, if done well, can be doorways to truths—the very truths that will restore peace to our souls. Perhaps it would be helpful to take time to peruse them, in art books, in Catholic stores, or on old Christmas cards. If you have an affinity for an image, that can create a bridge to a new relationship with the Blessed Virgin. Surely with artists around the world and over the centuries inspired to portray her in myriad cultural forms, everyone can find some image that will resonate.[18]

Use an image that catches your eye as a bookmark, or put it in a place where you can take time to just look at it. Talk to Mary, and beg her to heal your heart and to imprint her own loving gaze in your mind. Then when you seek maternal comfort, Mary has a reliable, concrete form.

When Elizabeth cried out, "Blessed is she who believed" (Luke 1:45), you were there! For what did Mary believe? She believed that the Almighty could do great things and that Our Lord's incarnation would destroy the power of death over us. That is the confidence of your spiritual mother, the one who takes you to her bosom with the greatest maternal affection. That is the love for which you were made and, if necessary, for which you may now be remade. Her foot has crushed the head of the serpent that has lied to you and harmed you previously.

Despite the fact that family wounds can be deep and complex—and wounds related to mothering are particularly devastating—they are not insurmountable. God wants us to be whole and at peace, and he has provided the means. It may take years of prayer and the sacraments, but that shouldn't deter anyone from beginning as soon as possible. Forgiveness is possible and essential to our spiritual growth. And since Our Lady is at the heart of our kinship, cast yourself into her arms and ask her to show you how to forgive.

CHAPTER SEVEN

Forgiving Our Children

We couldn't consider the difficulties that many women have with their parents without looking at what happens when our own children disappoint us. The starry-eyed affection we hold for our newborns can be gradually transformed as it becomes obvious that most are equipped with strong wills and determined ideas that very often conflict with our own. As the adage goes, we live life forward and learn it backward. Even when our children learn a lesson, it usually comes after some damage has been done.

Another maxim much loved by older women is "Little people, little problems," which may or may not be accurate. True, it is hard to sympathize with a ten-year-old's anguish over losing a school election when you've been through the trenches with an older child's out-of-wedlock pregnancy. But perhaps the smaller crises provide opportunities to grow in preparation for the larger ones. If only we could do things right the first time! So what do we do with these disappointments? Let's look at a few scenarios.

Drink and Drugs

Sarah and her husband had been faithful members of their parish, prayed regularly with their children, and discussed what they believed and why. When one son entered high school, they began to see some rebellion against their rules, but they took it in stride. Then as the months passed, he began to exhibit a variety of shocking behaviors, far removed from everything that he had been taught. He missed curfews, began shoplifting, argued about trivial things, was rough with his siblings, picked fights with his father, and refused to go to Mass.

Two years of tears culminated in a series of arrests, during which Sarah and her husband discovered a drug and alcohol problem that their son had hidden very well. The arrests were publicized, embarrassing all the members of the family, who were well-known in their parish and the local schools. While the young man didn't intend his behavior to hurt those he loved— addictions lead to a self-absorption that causes the person to ignore how his or her behavior affects others—each member of the family suffered in his or her own way.

Familiarizing themselves with the standard profile of addicted persons allowed the family members to understand why the boy acted as he did, but acts of forgiveness were necessary all the same. In fact, there is a temptation on the part of victims, when particular diagnoses or excuses explain why something has happened, to sidestep their grief or anger. It is as though diminished culpability undermines the justification for legitimate hurt. Obviously, the categorization of addiction as a disease is greatly helpful in the rehabilitation process, but the injuries addicts inflict on others still damage the relationships. That's why a good program for family members will encourage them to acknowledge their anger, disappointments, and suffering, which are very real. Whether or not the addict achieves sobriety or becomes capable of contrition, the family members must do their part in forgiving the actions that are objectively sinful, no matter the cause.

Poor Choices

Often parents and children have a great difficulty seeing eye-to-eye on lifestyle choices. When mothers dislike their daughter's choice of boyfriends, apparel, and creed, for example, the pain is usually as much personal as it is moral. Mothering is a vocation that absorbs our whole being, and thus when our children reject our advice, we receive it as a rejection of our very gift of self. Detaching in love is a very difficult challenge, but forgiveness must be at the heart of the matter.

Independence often involves stepping away from family influence, even at the risk of imprudence. How many daughters date the wrong young man out of a rebellious spirit, even when they know deep down that he is not the right sort of person! We could blame immaturity for the mistake, but the action is still objectively sinful.

Immodesty, impurity, irreverence, and a lack of filial piety are wrong, no matter what excuses can be found for toying with them. And excuses do little to shield a mother's heart from the rejection she feels in the face of this behavior.

After we forgive it will be easier to think clearly; it also becomes plain how much our egos are absorbed in the people our children become. We relish their successes, we mourn their setbacks, and we would love for them to be eye-catching billboards for our successful parenting techniques. This is only natural. Thus, when they stumble or take detours, it is possible that we are as much distracted by how others perceive their journey as we are for their well-being.

It's impossible to sort out completely the dynamics of family life. But we must do all in our power to remove ourselves from the equation and to see our children as God does. Their souls are what matter. The same mistakes that have purified and chastened us will take their course. The more we rely on prayer as our children's greatest resource in life, the closer we will be to our true calling.

Ingratitude

Another general category of suffering is caused by the arrogance and ingratitude that many children show toward the parents (and grandparents) who have sacrificed so much for them. A perversely humorous video went viral on the Internet recently. A father was livid over his teenaged daughter's Facebook rant against her parents. What galled him was her selfishness (just prior to her outburst, he had spent hours fixing her computer), her insolence (she deeply resented the few chores she was asked to do around the house), and her audacity (she posted a vulgar diatribe against her parents in a very public place). Therefore, in his own publicly posted video, he explained what the consequences would be in the home, then took a gun and destroyed her laptop in a hail of bullets. There would be no Facebook for her in the foreseeable future.

The fact that this video was seen and shared millions of times around the world might be an indicator of how it resonated with parents everywhere. Yet how many of us were insolent teenagers? How many of us knew far more than our poor, feeble parents? How many of us cringe at the memory of how we behaved before we matured? Each time one of our children sasses us, there should be at least some alarm bell deep in the cerebral cortex that reminds us that we did the very same and that hormones and ignorance go a long way in creating temporary monsters.

Sometimes that reminder can help to diffuse our anger.

Our children cannot know the difficulties of parenting, the daily—even hourly—decisions that need to be made, the isolation, the exhaustion, and the frustration that are the backdrop to so many years. Neither do they understand the naïve hopes we entertain that original sin and human freedom won't seriously disturb our family circle.

The answer is to forgive. Clear your decks mentally, so that you can continue to make prudent decisions, receive the wayward in love when they do come running, and be an example to your other children.

Teach Your Children Forgiveness

We started with the rocky years, but perhaps it's good to return to the cherubs who are still young enough to look to you for guidance and comfort. It is important to teach them how to forgive on a regular basis.

Norman Rockwell meant well, but he may have caused more confusion than he intended with his idyllic family scenes. Many a mother in her own home became convinced that hers was the only tribe of savages amidst an otherwise tranquil nation. Each was convinced that her own progeny had invented singular ways of tormenting siblings and friends heretofore unimagined.

When a child comes to you after being injured (whether physically or emotionally) it is good to hear him out, so that he can say why he feels hurt. Saying things like, "He didn't mean it," "Perhaps you misunderstood," or, "Don't be such a baby," are not helpful. Perhaps the other child did mean it, and perhaps he understood perfectly. Unkind actions—even misunderstandings—do hurt. Even adults experience this.

It might be better to say something like, "That hurt, didn't it?" or, "I'm sorry to hear that happened." Remind the child that when he's ready, he will need to forgive the perpetrator. Forgiveness doesn't need to be immediate, for you want to stress that it's not easy, but it needs to be done. Explain the procedure and, if appropriate, give him the words to say to the one who harmed him.

In the event that you have control over the child who harmed him, an apology should be forthcoming. And whenever anyone apologizes to your child, be certain that he responds with the words "I forgive you." So many will answer, "That's OK," which is not appropriate. What we want to teach our children is that uncharitable actions are not acceptable but must be forgiven. (It must be said that we should be forgiving these injuries along with our children—even if only silently from the periphery. Often the child has long forgotten the offenses that still fester in our maternal bosoms. Let them go!)

What our children need to learn is that they sin regularly, that others sin regularly, and that all can and must be forgiven. When injuries are received, they should consider the harms (sometimes scratches or bruised egos can instruct in ways that abstract lessons cannot) and resolve not to hurt others in a like manner. Children should be raised with a good vocabulary of vice and virtue, a familiarity with the need for forgiveness, and a steady reception of the sacraments—especially reconciliation.

A last thought concerns the nature of misunderstandings that often arise, especially in families. Although proximity can lead each person to think he or she knows what others intend by their words and actions, that's not always true. Occasionally our children will bring up memories in which they gravely misinter-preted our intentions. It's possible that they were terribly hurt by what they thought we said or by a somewhat distorted memory of events. These memories are especially painful when we meant to act kindly in a given situation or if the distortion puts an otherwise neutral event in a bad light.

As much as our children will need to forgive us our oversights, our failures, and our defects, it's grim to have such alterations of reality added to the bonfire of faults—especially when it casts our efforts in an even darker hue. If at all possible, I think it best to accept the memory as fact, since it has surely embedded itself into that child's consciousness, and to ask sincerely for forgive-ness without qualifications. When the healing is secure and the relationship is restored, there may be time to revisit the memory for the sake of accuracy, but it may be best to let it go. Surely we have made plenty of mistakes that they missed, overlooked, or forgot—and regardless, it will all be set right in heaven.

Two Lessons

Ultimately there are two important things to remember about the disappointments we experience in our children. Some inde-pendence of thought and action isn't sinful, and the child simply must act according to his own lights, no matter how much we "wasted" on piano lessons or sports equipment. Whether or not your child prays and is sincerely trying to discover God's will for his life, your wise opinions may be left unabsorbed. Chances are he doesn't see or fear the myriad difficulties that could be avoided if he accepted your direction. Forgive each child from the heart, and pray that he or she will discover a reliable path to God—for that's what it's all about.

The second important thing to remember is that sin bears its own seeds of destruction, "for the wages of sin is death" (Romans 6:23). No one will escape the consequences of ignoring God's laws. After we have sifted through our reasons for being angry or disappointed in our children's poor choices—is it the humiliation of personal rejection or real anguish over their souls?—we need to forgive the personal injury and confess our own pride. Then we need to pray in a firm but detached way, knowing that God is more anxious for their salvation than we are.

Sabrina was close to her grandmother, especially in the years leading up to the acrimonious divorce of her parents. The grandmother, who lived nearby, doted on her and offered a comforting haven for her several times a week. It was nice for Sabrina to get away from the ever-tense household in which arguments spilled over from day to day, each one triggered by the most innocuous of incidents.

Sabrina and her grandmother didn't often talk about what was going on in the family, which was a relief to the child, who was still in elementary school and unsure of how to express what she was feeling. Thus it came as a shock, when the topic was broached one day, to hear her grandmother say, "I will never forgive your mother for marrying your father. I *told* her not to do it."

The child didn't understand unforgiveness, the intransigence of children who defy their parents, or the pain associated with seeing loved ones make terrible choices. But as young as she was, she knew at the core of her being that she had just heard something inordinately harsh. And she knew that such an attitude was not helping the situation in her family.

It is entirely possible that Sabrina's grandmother foresaw that the marriage would be disastrous. In many cases the wisdom of the years brings insights that others cannot grasp, and legitimate concerns are ignored. Sabrina's mother may have married out of spite, out of a carefree whim that all would be well, or out of a sincere hope that she could change the man she had chosen into what he should be. Now she was reaping the consequences. She was scrambling to secure a job while trying to console her bewildered children and, amidst it all, suffering the emotional crisis of her own shattered hopes.

After the divorce Sabrina watched a macabre relationship develop between her grandmother and her mother. The older woman allowed her daughter to try to make amends through acts of oblation that she accepted as tributes to her wisdom. But there was never any indication that she had forgiven her daughter. The resentments simply sifted down to the ensuing generations.

No matter what your children have done, you need to forgive them. You are the beacon of faith in their lives, and you can shine brightly only if you let go of your disappointments and sorrows. There is no need to accommodate sin—and surely by now your children know your standards and morals—but we can strive to love them with the same tender love shown by the Blessed Mother, a love that brings out the best in others.

The lynchpin of that love is forgiveness. In forgiving the inevitable transgressions of your children, you can transform your relationships and help them to heaven. It's never too late.

CHAPTER EIGHT

Forgiveness Within the Church

Before one can discuss matters of the Church, it is important to understand the different dimensions of that word as understood by Catholics. The *Catechism* begins its explanation this way:

> In Christian usage, the word "church" designates the liturgical assembly, but also the local community or the whole universal community of believers. These three meanings are inseparable. "The Church" is the People that God gathers in the whole world. She exists in local communities and is made real as a liturgical, above all a Eucharistic, assembly. She draws her life from the word and the Body of Christ and so herself becomes Christ's Body (CCC, 752).

Most people are introduced to the Church on the parish level, with a particular priest responsible for the souls in a limited geographical area, but we must always be aware of the layered reality that this "local community" represents. As noted in chapter two, the Church is at once the spotless bride and the visible institution that bears the Petrine authority—through which we are guaranteed that what the Church teaches in terms of faith and morals is true. Only through prayer can we begin to understand how all of this works together in the way that *Dei verbum* explains:

> ...[I]n order to keep the Gospel forever whole and alive within the Church, the Apostles left bishops as their successors, "handing over" to them "the authority to teach in their own place." This sacred tradition, therefore, and Sacred Scripture of both the Old and New Testaments are like a mirror in which the pilgrim Church on earth looks at God, from whom she has received everything, until she is brought finally to see Him as He is, face to face (see 1 John 3:2).[19]

And yet the tension between the imperfect reality here and the perfection to which she is ordered is unavoidable, for the divine authority vested in the Church "to bind and loose," the trustworthiness of her teachings, and her potential for holiness are undermined by the constant and myriad failings of her members. For the institution is populated from top to bottom with sinners.

Mystical Realities in a Fallen World

Christ used strong words to explain the inevitable disparity between what spiritual leaders teach and how they live: "The scribes and the Pharisees sit on Moses' seat; so practice and observe whatever they tell you, but not what they do; for they preach, but do not practice" (Matthew 23:2–3).

And despite the "new and everlasting covenant" that would be created by the shedding of his own blood, he stressed:

> Do not think that I have come to abolish the law and the prophets; I have come not to abolish them but to

fulfill them. For truly, I say to you, till heaven and earth pass away, not an iota, not a dot, will pass from the law until all is accomplished.... For I tell you, unless your righteousness exceeds that of the scribes and Pharisees, you will never enter the kingdom of heaven. (Matthew 5:17–18, 20)

So the law stands, and the authority of the apostles and their successors remains, but so does this reminder that authority and holiness are not the same thing—and any serious student of history sees that the scandal previously offered by the scribes and Pharisees didn't end. Indeed, Christ's admonition on that particular point should reassure us that he completely understood this reality.

With this in mind, we must accept the fact that in any parish we will find the standard cross section of humanity, with defects and accomplishments, struggles and aspirations. To be sure, Christians may recognize their littleness before God and their need for God's help to be good (though not always), but the world, the flesh, and the devil are active as much within the Church's precincts as without—though usually in craftier disguises.

Surely the hope is that Christians—who profess to imitate the Word made flesh and who partake of the sacraments that bring divine life to their souls—would model virtuous behavior for others, but sadly that's not the case. Nothing justifies sin—ours or others—but we must not be shocked when our fallen nature eclipses our good intentions. It is only when we are familiar with both fallen human nature and existing supernatural realities that we can get past our unreasonable expectations and begin to deal with the scandal that flows from this duality.[20]

Suffering at the Heart of the Church

Vera was raised a Catholic and remained in the Church despite the breakdown of her marriage. She knew more than ever that she and her two children needed the sacraments, and within her vibrant parish she was always looking for good men to mentor her growing sons. It was this worthy intention that led her to help with the youth group, and when she met the dynamic new seminarian attached to their parish, she encouraged her sons to spend time with him and to help with his initiatives.

The boys took well to him at first, although they occasionally brought home some odd gifts and troubling language. Nothing was important enough to raise red flags until her younger son, Nathan, began to withdraw and fight going to the youth outings. Knowing that this could be age-related rebellion, Vera was reticent to draw conclusions until she noticed that he would also refuse to talk to the seminarian, who called the house often.

When another teenager in the youth group used subterfuge to try to pass information from the seminarian to Nathan, Vera realized that something was terribly wrong. Unfortunately, by that time Nathan's rebellion had become entrenched, and she was fighting his newly forming drug habits as well. It wasn't until years had passed and he had successfully completed a rehab program that the details of his molestation at the hands of the seminarian were finally revealed. Vera was crushed.

Adding to her heartbreak, when Vera took her allegations to the pastor, he was not only unsupportive but downright hostile. Perhaps he was frightened of the legal and financial ramifications that Nathan's molestation might have for his parish. At this time the scandal in Boston was unfolding, and there was no clear plan in place to deal with such things.

Imagine Vera's shock upon being told that the man who had assaulted her son wasn't actually a seminarian (despite his cassock and his introduction to the parish as a man studying for the priesthood). Rather he was merely a volunteer who had since disappeared.

Vera was entering a surreal world. What she had previously assumed to be true she was now told was false. Despite years of being a daily communicant, in the eyes of her pastor *she* was now the problem, and the sanctuary she had counted on her whole life would exclude her if she didn't back down. She was suspected of being a negligent parent and accused of looking for an opportunity to "make money" off the Church. She lost most of her friends, her longtime spiritual director, and all visible signs of support. She had placed her trust in things that she thought were entirely secure, only to discover that they were not. This was the heart of her suffering.

For years Vera clung to the Eucharist—which she had to receive in a neighboring parish—and prayed to the God who allowed all of this to happen. The years were dry, and the prayers were agony, but she knew that she couldn't walk away. She made it a point to make an act of forgiveness every morning, forgiving not only her priest and her bishop, neither of whom facilitated justice in her case, but also all the members of her parish who refused to believe her or help her in any way.[21]

Gradually Vera came to understand that she was a leper of sorts, giving flesh to one of the fiercest nightmares a parent can have concerning an innocent child. If her story were to be believed, then her friends would have had to face the dangers that surrounded their own children—despite their vigilance—and the fact that bad things can happen to faithful people in the very places they hope to find security. Her story would also stand as a reminder that the Church harbors all sorts of sinners, despite our desire to cast ourselves as the more virtuous members of society. Most of all, her tragedy would demand the introspection of all serious Catholics concerning the defects found within the Mystical Body of the Church on many levels.

When the world finally came to grips with the reality of the sexual abuse crisis, it reacted erratically—even incoherently—tarring wide swaths of the clergy as depraved while attacking the teachings of the Church on purity and chastity. Instead of prudence, there was a wild overreaction and suspicion by both clergy and laity concerning the other. While this will remain one of the dark chapters of our Church's history, Vera has healed enough to realize tremendous insights concerning the topic.

Interestingly, it was the kindness of a complete stranger that helped the healing process move along after years of silent suffering. Vera joined a faith formation class, and one of the new people she met there pieced together who she was. The woman came over to embrace her, saying, "I am so sorry I didn't do anything for you." The dam gates broke. There was a rush of consolation through which Vera could begin to forge friendships once more—though she admits that she will always be some-what guarded in this respect.

Many people around Vera are astonished that she didn't abandon her faith. Her witness proves that fidelity and forgive-ness amidst the most challenging circumstances will bring a tran-quility that cannot be explained in words. Jesus ministered to her himself, assuring her that "I will be enough for you," and he has been true to his word. Vera realizes that her abandonment was like his own in the garden before his unjust death.

While her son has his own path of forgiveness to walk, Vera has begun to use the wisdom gleaned from her difficult journey for the benefit of others. Her relentless insistence on a daily act of forgiveness is being rewarded with a quiet, rich communion within the shattered body of Christ. The *Catechism* speaks of this unity as the authentic heart of the Church:

> As sacrament, the Church is Christ's instrument. "She is taken up by him also as the instrument for the salvation of all," "the universal sacrament of salvation," by which Christ is "at once manifesting and actualizing the mystery of God's love for men." The Church "is the visible plan of God's love for humanity," because God desires "that the whole human race may become one People of God, form one Body of Christ, and be built up into one temple of the Holy Spirit" (CCC, 776, quoting *Lumen Gentium*, 9, 48; *Gaudium et Spes*, 45; Paul VI, June 22, 1973; *Ad gentes*, 7; see *Lumen Gentium*, 17).

Authentic communion comes at a great price. Just as the wine and the grain are pressed for the benefit of the one who needs to be fed, Christ laid down his life and asks us to imitate him. In her own way Vera followed the path of Ignatius of Antioch, who was led into the Roman Colosseum, saying, "I am the wheat of God. I must be ground by the teeth of wild beasts to become the pure bread of Christ."[22]

As each of us submits to that process in our own way, God mingles our blood and tears with his own. That is a sign of the true Church. In the words of C.S. Lewis:

... [T]he Church exists for nothing else but to draw men into Christ, to make them little Christs. If they are not doing that, all the cathedrals, clergy, missions, sermons, even the Bible itself, are simply a waste of time. God became Man for no other purpose....[23]

A Transcendent Vision

While Vera's story is one of betrayal that rises to the level of a crime, there are many Catholics who have been disappointed in their local churches over lackluster homilies, a dearth of formation programs, confusion over doctrine, and general human weakness. In these cases we must forgive and do what is possible to reconcile people to one another and to the truth.

A curious story about Noah and his sons may be instructive.

[Noah] planted a vineyard; and he drank of the wine, and became drunk, and lay uncovered in his tent. And Ham, the father of Canaan, saw the nakedness of his father, and told his two brothers outside. Then Shem and Japheth took a garment, laid it upon both their shoulders, and walked backward and covered the nakedness of their father; their faces were turned away, and they did not see their father's nakedness (Genesis 9:20b–23).

After this incident Noah blessed the sons who showed him honor, even in his debauched state, while he cursed Canaan, who would be the son of Ham (see Genesis 9:24–27).

There is a delicate balance between honoring the office of priest and defending the truth, which some clergy may obscure through their unfortunate words and actions. This is no justification for accommodating bad behavior—especially that which endangers the faith or well-being of the young—but it should provide a moment's pause about how to deal with what is beyond our control or what happened in the past. God sees all and is the final judge. We should tremble at the responsibilities of priests, all the while praying fervently and sacrificing generously for their fidelity to their duties.

Vera knew she needed the Eucharist; so do we all. Is it any wonder that those who have been entrusted with the Church's critical life-giving mission have been assaulted with temptations of every kind? If you have been harmed by members of the Church, pray for the grace to forgive, do what is necessary to restore communion among the various members of the Mystical Body, and consider ways to help deepen devotion to the truths of our faith. Reject the temptation to walk away in bitterness.

Although the baptized should know better, and those who teach the faith should live it more perfectly, our own sins remind us that we're all in need of God's grace. Furthermore, our faith tells us that we cannot do anything good without his help, nor do we offer God anything of worth except Christ himself and that which is done in his name. We must simply offer our own oblation of love along with that of St. Paul, who wrote: "Now I rejoice in my sufferings for your sake, and in my flesh I complete what is lacking in Christ's afflictions for the sake of his body, that is, the Church" (Colossians 1:24).

CHAPTER NINE

The Wounded Healer

One of Rumer Godden's most poignant stories, *Five for Sorrow, Ten for Joy*, centers on a convent of French nuns who minister to prostitutes. Theirs is a strict community of order and devotion, dedicated to bringing the healing balm of Christ to unfortunate women who have lost all sense of self and dignity. Within the group there is one question that isn't asked of the women: how they came to join. For there are two ways to enter the community.

The usual way is by a prompting of the Spirit; the less traveled path is being rescued from the street and wishing to live a life of reparation for oneself and others. Of course, any sister who deals directly with the wayward souls might know who came into the convent by means of the latter path, but discretion surrounding each vocation is sacrosanct. Surely God receives them all with the same tender love. This is a reminder that his magnificent image never leaves us.

A Difficult Beginning
Mary's start in life is not what anyone would want for a daughter. Her entire family was traumatized by her father, a fanatical Catholic who suffered deeply from mental illness. His behavior was erratic—quite violent at times—and he was unable

to support the family. They moved constantly because of their inability to pay their bills and even spent time on the streets. The parents separated when Mary was seven, and although her father was eventually institutionalized, the relationship was enough to instill in all his children an unhealthy fear of God.

With her mother working in the evenings, there was little supervision of the family. The youngest of five, Mary was protected in some ways by her siblings, but she lived in constant fear and had debilitating panic attacks from a very early age. When she was eight she was sexually molested by an acquaintance of one of her siblings. This added even more trauma to her already bewildering world, and her self-esteem plummeted.

This event marked the start of self-destructive behaviors that would only increase over the years. Mary became pregnant at the age of fourteen, and her mother insisted on an abortion. Her sister drove her to the clinic. All Mary remembers is the noise and the pain—shocking, horrific pain, as if her insides were being sucked out. Feelings of despair followed.

Two years later, Mary became pregnant again, and the procedure was repeated. Her mother told her the fetus was merely a clump of cells and that she had no choice but to be rid of it. Again her sister drove her. That horrible day ended with one of the worst panic attacks Mary had ever suffered. She thought she was in cardiac arrest.

But the attacks intensified, as did Mary's alcohol use and her promiscuity. Previously she had only been intimate with boyfriends, but now she began having one-night stands. Another pregnancy, and once more her mother and sister played their parts.

Nagging Guilt

Mary was engulfed in the darkness of depression and self-hatred. She felt dirty and ashamed. Despite the legality of abortion— which allowed her to think it was an acceptable choice—she was wracked with feelings of guilt. She couldn't bring herself to tell even her friends.

When she was twenty-three, Mary met a decent man. In time she became pregnant again, and they decided that they would like to commit themselves to each other and keep the baby. They married and were blessed with three lovely children.

But the guilt wasn't gone. Mary still suffered from panic attacks, she was deeply fearful that something would happen to her children as the price of her abortions, and her terror of large places led her to miss many social events and even milestones in her children's lives.

It was at this point that Mary's husband told her she needed to do something. He was also Catholic and knew about two of the abortions. They had agreed to raise the children in the Church, but although Mary had been baptized, because of her early family situation, she had not received the other sacraments.

While Mary's guilt and various fears kept her at arm's length from God, she did have a deep desire for those sacraments. Unfortunately, with a host of unresolved feelings about her past, even stepping into a church building would trigger a panic attack. Knowing it was time to face her past, she looked into faith-based programs that might help her to move forward.

Realizing that her abortions were at the heart of her problem, Mary first discovered programs that might help her deal with her abortions, which she knew were at the heart of her depression,

Mary first discovered a post-abortion Bible study offered by PACE.[24] She bonded with the other post-abortive women there. She was the first of them to embark on a Rachel's Vineyard retreat. On that retreat the real healing began. The program allowed her to face her decisions, to name the children she had lost, and to memorialize them in a fitting way. She learned that God is love and that his mercy will not be withheld from anyone. She who had assumed that she was destined for eternal condemnation felt God's embrace of love and received the forgiveness for which she so yearned.

As Mary told her story in that safe place, her own tears turned into healing waters. Thirty-five years of suffering ended with the gentle words of the priest who absolved her: "You poor child, you've suffered so long." The babies whose humanity she had denied for over three decades were released into the arms of God. Mary was free.

That retreat was followed by another, under the auspices of ACTS,[25] in which she made an inventory of those she still needed to forgive. Despite her father's behavior, which had tormented the whole family until his suicide when Mary was twelve, she found it more difficult to forgive her mother. Perhaps her father's diagnosis provided some excuse in Mary's mind; perhaps it was her mother's insistence on procuring the abortions and the surrounding neglect that Mary could never fathom, particularly once she had a daughter of her own. There was also the compliant sister and all who had lied to her about those "clumps of cells." They each needed to be forgiven for their complicity—as well as for their inability to comprehend Mary's subsequent suffering when she tried to explain it to them.

A particular exchange had an impact on Mary that has directed her ever since. At the end of the Rachel's Vineyard retreat, the women were paired, and each was asked to comment on the Christlike qualities of the other. When the other woman began to speak of her likeness to Mary, she fully expected her to continue with a word about Mary Magdalene. Imagine her astonishment when her partner related that she was like the Blessed Mother who suffered at the foot of the cross. Indeed, that was where she had remained—in sorrow over those dear souls whom she knew were made in the very image of the Son of God. The words penetrated Mary's soul, and she noted that henceforth "my misery became my ministry."

Mary has found tremendous peace in God's time and has done surprising things with her newfound joy. She gives her testimony publicly to large groups of people, in hopes of helping others avoid her mistakes. She has forged a spiritual tie with at least one young woman, who asked Mary to be her confirmation sponsor. Mary is finding her spiritual motherhood expanding according to the needs of the Spirit.

Mary also knits and crochets prayer shawls, which she donates to charity. And out of nowhere has come an overwhelming appreciation of the beauty of nature accompanied by a zeal for photography.

No doubt if you called your diocesan respect life office, you would be led to many other women whose stories are similarly courageous and hopeful. This harkens back to the story of the French convent. And that intriguing story is a revisitation of the Gospels, in which we hear of miraculous healings, sins forgiven, and lives transformed. Indeed, that is the very heart of our faith and the reason we cling to our Redeemer.

A New Identity in Christ

Those who deal with post-abortive women recognize a curious mindset that is all too common—that of the woman who has grown comfortable in her pain, has accommodated herself to being a victim, and fears healing, both because she feels she doesn't deserve it and because she would have to learn to live differently.

> This personal dynamic is ancient. Jesus himself encountered it when he healed people of blindness and physical deformities. The hypocrites attacked him as well as those who had been healed, spreading mistrust, focusing on the laws he had broken rather than being able to rejoice with the healer and the individual whose dignity had been restored and whose ailment had been removed. Their contempt covered their own trepidation about losing their power.[26]

The "power" of which these founders of Rachel's Vineyard speak is the power to control our own environment—maybe not all of it but the little things that remain in our hands. This desire for control is common to a variety of people: those living in codependent relationships, those with eating disorders, those who decide that God cannot forgive their particular sins, and those who use their defects as a way of controlling others. Changing one's identity from "victim" to "fully healed" would create a radically different landscape—the thought of which is more frightening for many than their present unhappiness.

If this fear sounds remotely familiar, then you need to bring it to God—preferably as he waits for you in the Blessed Sacrament.

Our Lord said repeatedly, "Be not afraid!" He came that you might have a life abounding in good things, for that was the express will of his Father:

> He destined us in love to be his sons through Jesus Christ, according to the purpose of his will, to the praise of his glorious grace which he freely bestowed on us in the Beloved. In him we have redemption though his blood, the forgiveness of our trespasses, according to the riches of his grace which he lavished upon us. (Ephesians 1:5–8)

Look at that language: *love, glorious, freely, riches,* and *lavished.* These are not the words of a God who begrudges us, who forgives out of duty, or who is formulaic in the demands of love. This is the language of a passionate God who is just waiting for our word—for our critical, free-will acceptance of a gift beyond measure. These are the marks of a Lover who will weep if the gift is rejected—one of the prime reasons for Our Lord's tears in the Garden of Gethsemane.

The directors of Rachel's Vineyard are all too familiar with the obstacles that some women place in the path of healing:

> As long as we can be pointing out what's wrong with everything around us, we never break through to humility, a place where God's blessing takes root because we surrender our control and allow the master painter to work on the canvas of our lives. The more we trust this master artist, the more He creates a picture that is magnificent and priceless. In addition, God actually

transforms the negative images and colors into things of great beauty....

This is what God truly desires to do in our lives, when we let go of our control and take the great risk to trust him—to make ourselves vulnerable, to share the secret, dark and ominous portraits that were painted on the canvas of our lives after destructive experiences, like abortion, sexual abuse and other deep personal violations.[27]

If we admit that sin offended God and harmed each of us—in whom his likeness rests—we have taken the first step to wholeness. Subsequently we need to receive forgiveness for each element of the sin, as Mary's testimony shows. We ask God's forgiveness, and we extend our own to those who sinned against us. Each void will then be filled with the abundance of God's mercy—transforming our lives in ways unimagined. The new identity is not something to fear but something to anticipate with joy.

We may have lost this ability to trust in the gifts of God, and even this step will require an act of faith: "Lord, I have never felt your love, but I believe it exists. Instead of good gifts, I have been handed stones. Now I trust that you will show me your goodness and fill my heart with joy."

Try to pray this prayer (or compose your own act of faith), and prepare to be led by the Spirit to that place where authentic healing and rejuvenation are possible. It is true that you do not deserve them, but none of us do! That is the marvel of the living and true God—that he wants them for us regardless, and is waiting to shower us with love.

CHAPTER TEN

Forgiving and Forgetting?

An important question that many well-meaning people will ask themselves after a bad experience is "Have I forgiven adequately?" or in other words, "How do I know if I've truly forgiven?"

This was touched upon in chapter six, where the priest told Leah that her lack of desire for revenge was an indication of her good will. But many struggle with their inability to completely put out of their minds what happened—as though this would be a reasonable sign of success. Despite concerted efforts to forgive, there are still negative memories attached to the persons who hurt them. Or a victim finds herself turning the harmful event over in her mind, wondering about its import.

It is entirely possible that one factor leading to this quandary is the trite phrase "forgive and forget." While this is good advice for little transgressions, such as the immature things done in childhood or when a mature person does something out of character, forgetting grievous injuries or ignoring a pattern of troubling behavior is virtually impossible—and might even be dangerous.

Shifting the Relationship

Beverly was married and pregnant with her second child when her parents divorced. Both her mother and her father were difficult people, but it was her mother's alcoholism that spun out of control and finally broke the marriage apart. Having nowhere else to go, her mother moved into Beverly's already crowded apartment. Remarkably, her parents continued to talk to each other, and they remarried a few years later.

The casualty in the family was Beverly, who was stunned to hear from her parents that *she* had been the cause of their breakup. As is usual with active alcoholics and the codependents who live with them, reality became distorted and the real problems were never addressed. Beverly was her parents' scapegoat.

In time, Beverly made the choice to detach from her parents and to grow beyond their defects. She and her husband looked for other couples to mentor them. This choice—which accompanied her closer embrace of her childhood faith and then her conversion to the Catholic Church—was fortified by prayer, the reading of Scripture, an appreciation for the other good gifts that God had bestowed in abundance, and the sacraments.

Years later Beverly's parents sought to renew their relationship with her, since they wanted to know their grandchildren. Their overtures were kind, but Beverly could see that nothing had changed. She invited them for visits and began to offer what turned out to be many long, difficult years of filial piety, which she considered her proper response to aging parents.

Did Beverly ever forgive? While she cannot remember any particular acts of forgiveness, she concludes that she began to make the "daily choice to shift the relationship." She understood that both parents came from highly dysfunctional backgrounds and that each was a slave to a disease that crushes relationships and the ability to take responsibility for one's actions. She pitied her parents' deep unhappiness and their chronic inability to find consolation in the joys of family life.

How does a victim know that she has forgiven? There seem to be two reliable guides.

First, she can say that she wholeheartedly wants what is best for the one who has harmed her. She doesn't have to remain in a particular relationship—many times the toxic behaviors of the other make that impossible—but she has no lingering resentments or hard feelings. She can pray for the other with sincerity and even make sacrifices with warmth and good will.

Second, she can begin to assess with maternal maturity what makes the perpetrator act as he or she does. This is not a knee-jerk form of excusing bad behavior or covering for others by taking the blame herself. (The latter is usually expressed in the horrid justification of domestic violence, "It was my fault he beat me—I burned his dinner.")

Beverly came to realize that her parents were difficult and unhappy because they had never forgiven the malicious things that they had suffered in their own early years. They harbored a bundle of resentments that they in turn projected against the world in general. While this didn't give them a pass to treat others badly, it explained why they acted as they did and why it was impossible for Beverly to make them happy. She wasn't the problem, only the conduit through which they vented their own deep sorrow.

What about forgetting?

As noted above, the small transgressions of everyday life are usually best forgotten, but the larger injuries are valuable remembrances. The key is what we do with the memories. One value they have is in the power of evangelization. If an incident can be related (without revealing the defects of another), then others can see that forgiveness frees an individual from resentment. This shows the marvelous beauty of letting go; actual events don't have to cripple people forever.

We often misunderstand the abiding peace exhibited by others, thinking that they haven't suffered as we have. Their stories might reveal that peace is possible despite injuries. Thus they provide hope to others.

There are other benefits. Remembering events as they happened—dispassionately, without exaggeration or pity—can allow us to make prudent judgments about how to proceed with a particular person. Beverly understands that her mother is broken in many ways, and thus she is guarded about what information she shares with her. She knows that confidences may not be kept, that her mother's reactions will often be erratic or cruel, and that thus some information is best kept away from the seemingly doting grandmother. For Beverly to force herself to forget these things would be to set herself up for repeated shocks or betrayals. In love she proceeds with great caution with a woman who has yet to face the reality of her own family history.

Stepping Outside of Time With God

Just as forgetting is unwarranted when someone chooses to maintain a relationship with a malicious person, forgetting is likewise impossible with a singular traumatic event. Amnesia isn't a normal trait in a healthy human brain, and forgetting such an incident would be more of an alarming indicator than a sign of grace.

A chance stroll past the television in her dormitory recreation room allowed Melinda to catch a glimpse of John Paul II, who was visiting the United States early in his pontificate. She stood transfixed as he watched Tony Melendez playing the guitar for him. The young man—a thalidomide baby born without arms—was playing the instrument with his feet. At the end the energetic young pope jumped off the dais to embrace him. This so touched the heart of the student, who had been raised Catholic, that she decided to offer herself however she could to her Church.

Interestingly, although she couldn't have known it at the time, the song that Tony Melendez sang to the Holy Father spoke of God's call to Melinda. It was a song about bringing God's light into the darkness. This is exactly what would transpire in her life ten years later.

Melinda began her new life by presenting herself at the Newman Center on campus and offering to clean the priest's house for free, though the staff insisted on paying her. During one of her housekeeping calls, as she was tidying the priest's bedroom, to her horror she found inappropriate videos. Repulsed and hoping to preserve her faith, she dropped that commitment and subsequently kept the priest at arm's length.

After insistent calls asking her to pick up her check, and against her better judgment, Melinda stopped at the rectory. There she found only a young man with whom she was somewhat acquainted. He had once been a seminarian and was now a volunteer at the center. In one bewildering, violent act, the large man grabbed her, threw her down on the living room floor, and brutally raped her.

Melinda's feelings of shock and betrayal almost overwhelmed her. Yet she was in the middle of finals, and as a resident assistant, she had to function for the sake of others. So she proceeded numbly through the next week, deciding not to report the incident for fear of scandalizing others about her beloved Church. Furthermore, she thought that pursuing justice would only increase her pain. With the AIDS epidemic newly absorbing the nation, she was mostly worried about contracting that dreaded disease, not to mention becoming pregnant.

Melinda returned home at the end of the semester and did all she could to put the matter behind her. As she turned it over in her mind, there was the haunting thought that she should have known better. Why had she ignored the nagging voice inside that told her not to go to the priest's home? Like many rape victims, she took responsibility for the crime against herself.

Melinda began exhibiting classic post-traumatic symptoms. She would obsess on particular details of the attack, she would cry every night, and most upsetting to her, thoughts of the attack would barge into her prayers, distracting her when she needed God the most. After ten years she finally talked to a Catholic therapist, who responded in an entirely healthy manner—expressing outrage at the event and reminding her that no woman deserves to be raped, *ever*. They discussed the enormity of the assault on her dignity, what the man had stolen from her, and how angry she had a right to be.

Melinda had never allowed herself those thoughts. She now found them essential in reframing the assault, so that she no longer felt complicit in the act. A priest gently took her back to the event through prayer. As terrifying as it was to be deliberately reliving the event, he asked her to look for God at that moment. To her astonishment, he was there. He was also on his back, being affixed to his cross next to hers! As they both lay there, he said, "This day you will be with me in paradise."

As overwhelming as this consolation was, there was more. The Blessed Mother, standing nearby, approached Melinda and lifted her gently, wrapping her own mantle around her shoulders and leading her away from the Newman Center.

Through this experience, Melinda was relieved of her fears and obsessions, but she knew she wasn't finished. There was still the forgiving process, which she now felt capable of approaching. The priest was available for this step as well. He asked her to consider a way to see the man who had assaulted her in a nonthreatening guise. For this Melinda reached into his childhood. The priest said, "Don't look at the degenerate, but forgive the little boy who was brought to such a deed." Melinda could easily see that innocent child, and her heart, repaired by God's own grace, was now fully capable of forgiving him.

Lest one think that this is sidestepping reality, we must remember that time is only a device that we have been offered to make sense of a deeply layered universe that God sees in his own omniscient way. We can enter more profoundly into reality with his help, especially when dealing with grace and mercy.

So again we raise the question concerning a person's ability to forget. Can such a horrific assault ever be forgotten? Is that what we actually expect?

Perhaps with a miracle of God, it could be forgotten, if he wanted, but that is not at all normal. Time can heal all wounds but not always in the straightforward way that we imagine.

Melinda's experience will always be with her in some form. Though it's far less painful and no longer debilitating, she has to be careful about the setting in which she discusses it, for it is still laden with emotion. But God's personal tenderness in reminding her of his presence is a gift she wants to share with all, for it wasn't unique to her moment of suffering. Thus, forgetting the incident would not only be curiously unusual but would deprive others of a deeper truth of God.

We should not ask for the ability to forget the sins against us but rather to remember them in a way that we can manage, that will give glory to God for his great mercy, and that will provide assistance to others in their darkest suffering. This both Beverly and Melinda are happy to do whenever possible. Their stories should give hope to others that one can walk through fire and be transformed, not consumed. "For with God nothing will be impossible" (Luke 1:37).

CHAPTER ELEVEN

Irreducible Complexity

Life isn't always simple; neither is forgiveness. Some difficult situations pose a conundrum, requiring careful analysis to distinguish paths of healing. There are often myriad shortcomings that contribute to conflicts and misunderstandings, and thus freedom must accrue through prayerful discernment and stark honesty. Remember, though, that the Lord stands ready to help in this important process.

Breaking Down the Big Picture

While motherhood offers incomparable joys, it also brings with it the most wrenching sorrows because of parental bonds forged in love and expectation. Our children's journeys through life are extensions of our own, providing built-in roller coasters of emotion. Nancy found this out the hard way when her oldest daughter, Laura, developed bulimia while away at college.

Since she was far from home, Laura's difficulties weren't evident to her family for nearly a year, and their revelation stunned her mother. Nancy's first reaction was to blame herself for missing the signals. Then she struggled to discern other elements that may have led to the eating disorder. She thought about Laura's high school friends, many from wealthy families that seemed to prioritize external attributes, and a particular friend whose narcissism may have had a deleterious effect on Laura. The stoicism of Nancy's husband may have inhibited his ability to show paternal affection. Why hadn't Nancy stepped in like a good mother to preserve her daughter's healthy formation?

As she mulled over the situation, she realized that there was more to it than just the particular family and neighborhood deficits. She extended the blame to the Catholic Church and to the particular Catholic school that Laura had attended. In her experience, neither had proactively supported parents trying to instill virtues in their children, and both seemed to have failed in combatting the tide of immorality in the popular culture. Nancy had several Protestant friends whose pastors preached robust sermons on the topic of modesty and supported vibrant youth groups dedicated to living the Christian life. It seemed as though having such a reliable moral bulwark would have helped Laura cope with the issues of self-esteem and body image.

Nancy had to also consider the misguided feminist movement at large, which in its struggle for equality and dignity had swerved into championing promiscuity and the objectification of women. Its platform of empowering women had a profound effect on the fashion industry. Not only were the models living very unhealthy lives in order to make themselves bone-thin, but there was also the widespread editing of images to make models look even slimmer. The young were exposed to these doctored images, confusing boys about what women should actually look like and leading many girls to despair.

Nancy found that she was quietly simmering, nursing resentments against her husband, against Laura's needy friend, against her pastor and the bishop, against school administrators, and against modern culture as a whole. But most importantly, she was angry with herself. She wanted to rewind the past and try to raise Laura differently so that this particular problem could be averted. In her second chance at motherhood, she would stress where a woman's true beauty lies and renounce with more vigor the airbrushed lies fed to young women. How could she forgive herself for having overlooked so many red flags over the years?

Alas, we don't get second chances. We must deal with our broken world and God's permissive will, which allows these things to happen.

Since there is resentment and injury—indeed, the injury to Laura has caused Nancy to suffer as well—Nancy must forgive. When she heals enough from this ordeal, it is possible that she will be a beacon for others who suffer in similar circumstances. And yet how to proceed with such a plethora of swirling thoughts!

Forgiving Piece by Piece

One begins logically by breaking the story into its components. We know already that it's less important to know the precise intention of the other than the perceived injury or slight. So Nancy must look at how she understood others should have acted. If her husband appeared to be less demonstrative than she liked, then she must forgive what she perceived as his shortcoming. The same applies to various priests and teachers and ultimately to the bishop, whom she thought could have helped in forming her children.

As Nancy considers all those whom she considered deficient in some way, she can turn each one over in her mind and process what she perceives to be his or her contribution to her injury.

When she understands as many angles as possible, she must begin her acts of forgiveness, stating firmly to herself that she forgives that person for his or her portion of her injury. When the words have been said, the sacrament of confession follows— so that the sins of resentment and bitterness are absolved and grace can begin its healing work in Nancy's soul.

Lastly we come to Nancy's own part in the problem, for which she admits being filled with regrets. In popular parlance many speak of the difficulty of "forgiving oneself" for oversights or misguided actions, but as Catholics we must be careful to avoid this imprecise language. In order to forgive ourselves, it would be necessary to compartmentalize ourselves into perpetrator and victim, which is impossible. There is no completely innocent part of ourselves that has the right to stand as judge—or as God!—in order to absolve the remainder; nor can we condemn ourselves, as though particular transgressions were beyond the redemptive action of Christ.

While people speak in this way with the best of intentions and the purest of motives, the language obscures a twofold notion of sin. The first element implies that the person has high enough moral standards to understand that the action or failings were wrong. Often these self-condemnations include thoughts like "I should have known better" and, "I can't believe I really did that." The second part is contingent on the first. Since the person believes that she has either a well-formed conscience or a higher standard of conduct, then she concludes that the failing is particularly egregious in the eyes of God, and the sinner must be held bound. Thus she cannot "forgive" herself.

It is true that the culpability for a mortal sin hinges on knowing that an action was wrong. But if one erred before understanding its implications, the knowledge later acquired doesn't add to the culpability. It only underscores the fact that God is right in his commands and that he wants us to be good for our own benefit.

Furthermore, it is essential to recall the ways in which we are damaged by sin: Our intellect is darkened, our passions are disordered, and our will is weakened. Therefore it is in our best interest to submit to God's light, his order, and his healing path of truth. The *Catechism* explains:

> Because man is a *composite being, spirit and body*, there already exists a certain tension in him; a certain struggle of tendencies between "spirit" and "flesh" develops. But in fact this struggle belongs to the heritage of sin. It is a consequence of sin and at the same time a confirmation of it. It is part of the daily experience of the spiritual battle. (CCC, 2516)

We are parts of the human race, which has been thus compromised. We are like St. Paul, who wrote, "I do not do the good I want, but the evil I do not want is what I do" (Romans 7:19). He certainly had high moral standards and a firm intention to follow Our Lord, but he was honest in facing his own defects, which were daily manifest. It should be noted that he never spoke of the need to forgive himself but only of the need to accept the redemptive sacrifice of God on his behalf.

Honesty With Ourselves Leads to More Honesty
Nancy has come far in her journey of forgiveness; she must now take it to its logical conclusion. She has forgiven her husband without determining whether or not he knew of his error; likewise

the school administrators and the chancery staff. Whether each should have been better informed and whether they acted in good will, she has determined, is irrelevant. The same goes for herself. If she is going to be harder on herself and hold herself to a higher standard than she expects of others, perhaps she is guided more by pride than by humility.

If Nancy does discover neglect (or another concrete deficiency) on her part, then she has sinned, and she must name that sin in confession. Many of us have been forced to revisit grievous (or stupid) errors that we cannot believe we made. We must humbly admit that, indeed, we did those reprehensible things. To deny our ability to sin is to deny the truth of our existence. God came precisely to save us from ourselves, and to say we don't need him is an insult born of pride. This pride is only compounded when we refuse God's grace by implying that our standard of behavior is higher even than his own.

This painstaking work of studying an injury, breaking it into small, manageable portions, and then shedding the light of sacramental grace on each facet brings about both healing and clarity. The burden of bitterness and anger is lifted, so the one who was too filled with resentment to love effectively is now freer to respond with gestures that are actually soothing to those around her. Furthermore, once the hostility subsides, she is free to assess the entire situation more calmly.

In Nancy's case it is entirely possible that her view of her husband and various priests will undergo a transformation. She may note an important truth: that her other daughters—loved by the same father and struggling through the same toxic culture—don't have any traces of body-image issues or eating disorders.

She may remember that priests have an enormous challenge to preach to a very wide stratum of parishioners on any given Sunday—devoted daily communicants along with those whose ties to the Church are precariously fragile. Additionally, she could weigh the fact that those Protestant friends who have wonderful youth groups promoting modesty do not have sacramental confession to restore a right relationship with God when they have transgressed his commandments.

As with many who have suffered from a health issue or trauma, both Nancy and Laura may one day be called to minister to others who suffer. Their time in this valley of darkness can actually be a source of insight and hope for those who follow similar trajectories. Nancy's difficult sojourn through self-recrimination before receiving God's liberating absolution will yield a lamp along the path for others, for it is a common detour en route to the Divine Embrace.

Truly, nothing is wasted, including peripheral effects of sin that touch members of the family. This is yet another indication that the trials we endure can result in deeper faith and a more powerful illumination of God's truth. Our Lord knows our good intentions as well as our shortcomings. He loves us no less for our myriad defects.

In that light perhaps we should call to mind the first time we held our dear children. Recall that as we kissed those downy heads, those precious babies had done nothing to merit our gratuitous affection. Even now we cannot earn God's love, for it surrounds us unbidden, no matter what we do. Receive that love—and the grace that brings life to our souls—for any good that we intend is his anyway.

CHAPTER TWELVE

Peeling Away the Layers

While a lifetime of difficulties might take years to work through, even a single incident may not be as straightforward as it first appears, and forgiveness will be a layered process that will need constant attention. For the sake of an example, let us imagine the terrible misfortune of a child being hit by a car while very young. Perhaps she was around six and riding a bicycle in her cul-de-sac when a teenaged neighbor carelessly headed out to work, turning his short commute into her long years of suffering.

The Long Road

As the girl comes through her surgeries and the immediate crisis, she faces the stark reality that she can no longer walk. School will be a challenge, there will be many games in which she cannot participate, and she may suffer residual pain from the accident. Still, with the creative love of her family, the sincere sorrow of the young driver, and the young girl's nascent faith, it is entirely possible for her to completely forgive the young man. With grace she can adapt to this new world and even find happiness in surprising things.

But ten years later it may hit her that she will never dance with her friends and that dating will be complicated. Some young men might confuse their concern with pity, or their discomfort with her condition might outweigh the pleasure of her sunny personality. The complications grow in ways that a six-year-old could never have imagined. Each loss will require a new act of forgiveness as her injury manifests itself in ways she didn't foresee.

Ten years hence the young woman may have found a life's mate, yet she realizes that she won't walk down the aisle. The regret over the loss of this sentimental wedding image might shock her, given that she knew all along that it would be impossible. Conversations about children will be colored by the sober truth of her condition. Her ongoing acts of forgiveness will have to include these losses as well.

Later in life there may be medical complications—perhaps scoliosis or other orthopedic challenges that age exacerbates. She may be limited in offering assistance with her husband's growing infirmities, and she may feel like a burden on others as the years pass. Once again she must forgive the young man's inattention and God's permissive will, lest she descend into bitterness.

Many if not most injuries will need to be peeled off in layers. After the initial act of forgiveness, the quieter, calmer vantage point may actually reveal new aspects of the event that were previously overlooked—some of which may inflame fresh sorrow or anger. These facets will take time to process and then be put aside through subsequent acts of forgiveness. Some dimensions may be quite surprising, and the overarching lesson may be to understand both the complexity of the human person and his or her ability to put up layered defenses. If one is to love with abandon, these defenses will eventually have to come down and be replaced with layers of trust in God's consolations:

> Blessed be the God and Father of our Lord Jesus
> Christ, the Father of mercies and God of all comfort,
> who comforts us in all our affliction, so that we may
> be able to comfort those who are in any affliction, with
> the comfort with which we ourselves are comforted by
> God. For as we share abundantly in Christ's sufferings,
> so through Christ we share abundantly in comfort too.
> (2 Corinthians 1:3–5)

We will have consolations, not only for ourselves but to bring to others. This promise is reliable and indicative of God's marvelous generosity. But forgiveness must become a way of life. This disposition will be strengthened and sustained through sacramental graces.

Like Ripples in a Pond

There is an entirely different way to look at layers, and this would be in relationship to the persons involved in any particular transgression. A better word, though, would be ripples—for these begin with those closest to the injury and move outward.

For the sake of continuity, we will continue with the example from above. We'll assume that both the teenager and the injured girl are loved by several family members and that the families know each other and are known to the wider community. Indeed, everyone surrounds both families with loving support, prayers, and thoughtful gestures of concrete aid.

While the young girl was most harmed by the accident and has the greatest task of ongoing forgiveness before her, her parents also must forgive the boy. Their acts of forgiveness should gently guide their daughter, but they must be sensitive to her suffering and not intimidate her in any way. To forgive wholeheartedly is good, but if she is struggling, they certainly won't be overly affectionate with the boy, as it could cause her to think that they are indifferent to her pain. In prayer they will feel their way through the substantial task of healing to restore as much unity to the community as possible.

The parents of the driver also have their part to play. They must let go of their anger over the boy's action and how it has impacted their lives. Likewise each person affected—siblings, grandparents, and others—should forgive to the degree that the accident affected his or her life.

The young man's contrition will no doubt last throughout his life. Knowing that everyone has forgiven him and that he is loved will make the difficult years ahead more bearable.

Apart from the immediate circle, a curious situation often arises in which members of the wider group rush in to forgive the offender in a way that seems offensive to the real injured parties. This happens on occasion in the news, when teenagers have harmed someone, or a priest has been accused of sexual impropriety, or a coach or teacher is being dismissed amidst scandalous rumors. Many times friends and coworkers publicly announce their love and support for the suspected perpetrator— which is certainly understandable—but then go on to forgive his transgressions and suggest that everyone else do likewise. Often they will toss out a line of Scripture or a reminder that Jesus said to forgive (and not to judge!), which only confuses the issue.

If we look at the rippling effects of an injury, we must admit that those more removed from an injury really have little to forgive. In the case above, they are not wheelchair-bound, their dreams for their child are not shattered, and they will not have to visit a son in prison or frequent doctors' offices for years to come. In the case of sexual scandal—whether of a clergyman, a teacher, or someone else entrusted to build character in children—those speaking of their good qualities shouldn't dictate how others proceed through the forgiveness process. Their lives were not compromised by the person in question.

The farther one is from the immediate harm, the more carefully he or she must phrase a response to the transgression. We cannot judge the motives of others, and in most cases we don't have all the details concerning an interaction, but statements of support must not blur the difference between excusing and forgiveness. Few are called to actually judge the actions of others, and the rest are left to seek discretion in how they respond to events.

It is the actual victims who must undertake the hard work of forgiveness, which requires prayer, gentle guidance from trusted souls, a careful assessment of each component, and God's healing grace. Those who are unfamiliar with the process cannot be pushed into it with pious admonitions. Christ scored his own words on the matter in blood, and without gentle, trusted assistance grounded in his love, one is hard pressed even to know where to begin. Forgiveness is precisely what is needed, but its messenger can make all the difference.

CHAPTER THIRTEEN

The Wider Picture

As deeply personal as the wounds of sin can be, in many cases they are part of a wider trend of injustice, such as war, ethnic violence, or embedded cultural prejudices. The tragic parade of centuries illustrates for us the darker side of mankind, which so often gives rise to the worst impulses. When we systematically refuse to honor God, sin embeds itself in the very fiber of society, as the *Catechism* explains:

> Thus sin makes men accomplices of one another and causes concupiscence, violence, and injustice to reign among them. Sins give rise to social situations and institutions that are contrary to the divine goodness. "Structures of sin" are the expression and effect of personal sins. They lead their victims to do evil in their turn. In an analogous sense, they constitute a "social sin." (CCC, 1869)

Men, women, and children suffer in myriad ways, which can make it hard to maintain the virtue of hope. In the words of one wry folk poem,

> *For men must work, and women must weep,*
> *And the sooner it's over, the sooner to sleep.*[28]

Yet amidst it all we must remember the demands of our faith.

Caught in the Maelstrom of Colonialism

Tom Cholmondeley, a British aristocrat, was heir to the vast Soysambu ranch, one of the largest in Kenya. Sarah Njoya lived on a scorched quarter acre nearby with her husband, Robert, and their four sons. Tragedy struck both families when Tom shot and killed Robert, whom he discovered poaching on his land. It wasn't the first incident of its type: Tom had previously killed a black man he believed to be a trespasser—one who turned out to be a wildlife ranger working undercover to investigate illegal activities in the area.

Racial tensions generally ran high in Kenya, as long centuries of colonial injustice had yet to be healed. Now they were spilling over in the region because Tom's previous case had been summarily dismissed. Then there was the particular fact that Tom's great-grandfather was responsible for carving enormous farms out of the Rift Valley, which had been home to the Masai tribe, the ancestors of the Njoya family.

It would have been easy for Sarah to get swept up in the drama. She and her fatherless boys could be cast as symbols of injustice and oppression through whom many could vent their long-standing, deeply felt frustrations. Whatever temptations she may have felt—and she was keenly aware of how much the blacks suffered in the current climate—Sarah refused to be used for political purposes.

Her maternal heart immediately reached out to Tom's parents, whom she knew to be grieving deeply. "I know what it feels like to lose a loved one. Being a prisoner is halfway similar to being dead," she said. She was relieved that the charge was reduced from murder to manslaughter, removing the possibility of the death penalty. She said firmly, "I would not want to see a death used to avenge my husband's own…. My husband died a painful death that could be avoided. But people make mistakes. Let's forgive, forget and move forward."[29]

Conflicts Born of Hatred

Many people over the centuries have been trapped in similar events—the "troubles" of Northern Ireland, the Rwandan massacres, and countless other internecine conflicts around the globe. In each case one has the choice of being a pawn subject to the expectations of the group or of reaching for the freedom made possible by forgiveness.

Miriam and Eva Mozes were Romanian twins chosen for Dr. Mengele's horrific medical experiments at Auschwitz. He used them as human guinea pigs, deliberately injecting them with various toxins to measure the effects. They both survived but returned to their village at the end of the war to discover that their entire family had perished. Miriam would die in 1993 from cancer of the bladder, a consequence of the Mengele experiments.

Eva meanwhile moved to Indiana, where she reached out to other victims of these experiments so that they could document their trauma. In 1993 she was asked to address a group of doctors in Boston. The request included a challenge: to copresent with a Nazi who had helped perform those experiments. Eva accepted the challenge, making the acquaintance of Dr. Hans Munch, who treated her with great courtesy. Indeed, when she asked about his memories of that time, he said that the death camp was "a nightmare he dealt with every day of his life." They devised a plan to make a joint visit to Auschwitz, where they would read a prepared statement.

Exactly fifty years after the liberation of Auschwitz, Eva and Hans stood with their families at the gates of the former prison and jointly signed a letter in which the doctor expressed his regrets and Eva expressed her forgiveness—not only of the contrite doctor but of Dr. Mengele himself. This she had never believed herself capable of doing. Afterward she noted, "As I did that I felt a burden of pain was lifted from me. I was no longer in the grip of pain and hate; I was finally free." Furthermore, she privately made an act of forgiveness of her own parents, whom she had hated for not saving her from her fate.

Eva knows that other concentration camp survivors despise her for her actions, calling her a traitor. But this is precisely an example in which the larger picture—with its stark contrasts between dark and light—can become its own prison. Interestingly, Eva calls forgiveness her "chemotherapy," for it was an act that healed and empowered her after years of considering herself a victim.[30]

Dying for Christ

One wave of persecution that has grown in the third millennium is that of anti-Christian violence. In many places around the world—especially in the Middle East—Christians' church buildings are destroyed, their homes pillaged, their children kidnapped, and their very presence decried. Many have had to leave communities that their ancestors settled centuries ago. Although their leaders beg for justice and attention from the international community, the persecution continues. Each loss entails a scarred heart.

Still forgiveness must be pursued—personally, deliberately, and sincerely. It is not an easy task when a community pools its pain, but God's command remains.

One young Muslim woman in Saudi Arabia found Christ through Internet chat rooms. Fatima Al-Mutairi was a twenty-six-year-old woman when she was drawn to the healing message of the Gospels. She wrote passionately of her newfound faith:

> Leave us to live in grace until our time comes
> My tears are on my cheek and, oh! the heart is sad
> On those who became Christians, how you are so
> And the Messiah says: blessed are all the persecuted
> And we, for the sake of the Messiah bear all things.[31]

Fatima's country, the very cradle of Islam, takes seriously its call to punish all who apostatize. Members of her family worked specifically for the government agency entrusted with that task.[32] Thus Fatima was entirely aware of the risk her conversion entailed. But she also knew the demands of Our Lord:

> Enough, your swords do not concern me at all
> Your threats do not concern me and we are not afraid
> By God, I am for death, a Christian, oh my eye
> Cry for what has passed in a sad life.
> I was far from the Lord Jesus for many years
> Oh history record and bear witness, Oh witnesses!
> We are Christians walking on the path of the Messiah
> And take from me this information and note it well
> Where is the humanity, and love, and where are you
> And my last words I pray to the Lord of the worlds
> Jesus the Messiah, the light of the clear guidance,
> That he changes your notions and [sets] right the scales
> of justice
> And spreads love among you, oh Muslims.[33]

Fatima knew her martyrdom was quickly approaching, and yet she spoke of her hope that those who seemed intent on her destruction would find that love as well. She had taken on the mind of Christ and had no room in her heart for hatred or vengeance—despite what surrounded her. Eventually, having been locked in her room by her angry brother, she wrote one last note to her friends, ending with, "The Lord is with me. He is my light and salvation, so from whom do I fear?" (see Psalm 27:1). Indeed, there was no trace of rancor in any of her words that day.

Shortly afterward her brother went into her room, cut out her tongue, and burned her to death, as news reports detailed.[34] Such was his duty as he understood it—to preserve the honor of his family and to punish her for abandoning Islam. No Christian in that setting could have expected any less.

Fatima exemplified the remarkable joy and courage of many who are currently suffering persecution. Her martyrdom was in the finest tradition of the earliest Christians who professed their faith forthrightly as they were put to the sword. Forgiveness was on their lips, and love prevailed in their hearts, even under duress and as they watched their companions being slaughtered all around them.

Courageous Christians of ancient Rome won a victory for Christ through their culminating acts of forgiveness. No doubt the firm witness of persons like Sarah Njoya, Eva Mozes, and Fatima al-Mutairi will have their effects.

Overcoming Cultural Prejudices

While some injustices lead to violence and death, others don't leave physical marks. Our recent American history showcases deep-seated prejudices that have alienated the descendants of slaves in particular but also waves of immigrants as they began the difficult work of assimilation. The Irish, the Germans, the Italians, and the Asians all had to prove themselves and endure injustices in school, on the job, and in society at large.

Furthermore, as the popular television series *Mad Men* reveals, in the decades after World War II, it was often extremely hard for women to be taken seriously in the workplace. It didn't help matters that their efforts to pursue professional careers were coupled with the technology and mindset that allowed the sexual revolution to take off. Their objectification and their subjection to residual prejudices—even rampant misogyny in places—led to abusive treatment to which they may have contributed in their own moral confusion.

While prejudice may explain the motivations of some who sin against charity, the explanation isn't necessarily helpful to its victims. Being one wounded person in a sea of injustice may accelerate feelings of despair, and making an isolated act of forgiveness may seem inadequate compared to the collective harm. Despite these obstacles and temptations, one must still forgive.

The choice of forgiveness is deeply personal, and no wider narratives—especially those including injustice or discrimination—should force its characters to drown under their toxic, impersonal tides. We haven't been created to travel in herds, despite being social creatures who drift easily into passing trends. Forgiveness is a blessing for those ready to pursue it, offering liberation from the very cultural shackles that can lead a people to spiritual ruin.

CHAPTER FOURTEEN

Repaying the Debt

It is extremely important to understand that forgiveness doesn't mean that one may not pursue the avenues of justice after a crime. According to the late Fr. John Hardon, sj:

> ...Justice is the virtue by which a person gives whatever is due, due first to God, due to others, and unexpectedly, even due to oneself....
>
> If we were to summarize the meaning of divine justice in the Old Law, it would be very simply synthesized in the Ten Commandments. The Decalogue is a summary of the divine justice. This God demands that his own rights be recognized and, by his rational creatures, lived up to, and then that the rights of other people be recognized and correspondingly practiced.[35]

Authority is necessary for justice to flourish, for without it there would be chaos. Furthermore, a legitimate authority will protect a people's right to honor the first three commandments, which concern the practice of religion, and the remaining commandments, which establish a just moral foundation for society. Justice enables society to run smoothly and its members to live in safety and harmony, even while sin abounds.

Tragedy Strikes

Anthony Walker was a bright seventeen-year-old, one of six children in a devout Christian family living near Liverpool, England. After he and his girlfriend spent an evening with his family, he and his cousin walked her to the bus stop. There they were surrounded by a violent gang who set upon them, ultimately killing Anthony.

The assailants were found and brought to trial. Despite the frenzy that surrounded the case—the gang members were white and seemed to have targeted the young couple because they were black—Anthony's mother was calm in her grief. When the men were found guilty, she was asked for her thoughts and answered, "Do I forgive them? At the point of death Jesus said I forgive them because they don't know what they did. I've got to forgive them. I still forgive them. My family and I still stand by what we believe: forgiveness."

Her forgiveness didn't change what she anticipated as the verdict. "It has been real hard going, but I feel justice has been done. I'm sure they will get the maximum sentence."[36] No one disputed her combined tasks of forgiving while holding the culprits accountable for their actions.

In yet another tragedy, a nun in the Kandhamal district of Orissa, India, was raped during anti-Christian riots in 2008. She demanded justice—not simply as a form of personal retribution but for the sake of the people she was working with. Having witnessed the inaction of the police during her assault, she knew that she needed to insist that the legal system act properly. Furthermore, being educated and well-formed in her faith, she had the resources to press forward to make the case for justice. While forgiving her attacker, to have neglected this element would have been to ignore the rights of the larger community.[37]

It is necessary to remove violent gang members from the streets and to lock up rapists. Neither Anthony's life nor the sister's bodily integrity could be restored in this life by incarcerating the guilty, but other lives could be saved and other women preserved from vicious and traumatic assaults by pressing forward with these cases. In neither instance was revenge or hatred part of the motive of the prosecution.

Sadly, at present many people feel re-victimized by the very justice system that is supposed to help them. They find few opportunities to influence the process. What may be most beneficial is a course of action that concretely recognizes their trauma, personalizes their quest for justice, and contributes to their ability to heal.

Apart from how well victims will cope in subsequent years, there are also questions concerning the guilty who must spend time in prison for their crimes. What will they find there? Will they come to repentance? Will they ever understand the actual consequences of their wicked actions? Or will they have only an abstract notion that they transgressed a law?

Restorative Justice
Anne Marie Hagan's father was brutally killed during a frightening confrontation with a mentally ill neighbor. Her father was only fifty-six. Anne Marie, a nineteen-year-old nursing student, was also injured by the axe-wielding man. The year was 1979, and shortly thereafter, she says, "I became completely consumed with anger, bitterness, vengeance, and self-pity."

Years later, in 1996, the justice system where she lived invited her to take part in a program called "restorative justice." She was encouraged to meet with the incarcerated man, who by that time was close to release. He wept and apologized, and she discovered that her previous resolve simply broke down.

> ...[I]n that face-to-face meeting, which lasted 1 hour and 40 minutes, 16 years and 10 months of misery was just wiped away. As he started to cry and said, "I'm to blame, I'm to blame," I couldn't take it anymore. I rushed around the table and hugged him, telling him that I forgave him. I remember saying to him, "Blame is too strong a word, blame is too strong a word."
>
> I could never have imagined that in doing so, I would set myself free. Finally I was able to let go of all the pain and torment that had held me captive, realizing that I'd been my own jailer. My life changed as I began to see the world through new eyes. I felt joy again, the numbness was gone.

Anne Marie has become a motivational speaker, and she talks about the freedom found in forgiveness.

> My father's killer is now 59 years old. He has a job, and he's working towards a university degree. I admire him for having the strength and the courage to rebuild his life. I visit him regularly. We have talked at length about what happened on that fateful day, and how my forgiving him has changed both our lives.

Not only has Anne Marie found freedom, but her spiritual motherhood has expanded in a way that she could never have imagined. "Before I forgave my father's killer, I had zero compassion for such people. Now I see each inmate as somebody's child."[38]

Finding the current criminal codes and correctional system woefully unhelpful from a human perspective, more and more communities are looking into ways to apply restorative justice, which has a deeply personal approach to crime. It is not meant to short-circuit justice or to replace existing laws but to add a healing dimension for those touched by criminal activity. An explanation of the program is furnished by Justice Fellowship, an offshoot of the late Chuck Colson's Prison Fellowship:

> Restorative justice is a practical, biblical approach to the problems of crime and punishment in our society. While it has foundations in the Old and New Testaments, it is not just a Christian concept. Restorative justice is indigenous to many cultures around the world and has been practiced for millennia.
>
> The principles of restorative justice are simple. Restorative justice recognizes that crime harms people. It does not simply break a law. The justice system should aim to repair these injuries. Crime is also more than a matter between the government and an individual offender. Since crime victims and the community bear the brunt of crime, they, too, must be actively involved in the criminal justice process.[39]

Rather than looking at crime as simply a legalistic matter with a prescribed punishment, those applying restorative justice focus primarily on who has been harmed. The victim of the crime is at the center of the process, for it is his or her life that has been impacted by the actions of the other. When that person has been determined, the next consideration is how to address the harm and who is best able to repair it.

Restorative justice requires that the offender be brought to understand how his action personally affected his victim—a need that is often addressed in victim impact statements, which are even now read before sentencing. Besides being faced with the pain he caused, he should be given a punishment proportional to that pain, as well as the appropriate tools to overcome any defects that may have driven him to act as he did. Furthermore, while he is incarcerated, he should be treated with dignity, and rehabilitative resources should be made available to him.

Finally, the needs of the community must also be considered, since crime usually has a wider effect than just the families of the perpetrator and the victim. These harms need to be taken into consideration and weighed as the convicted move toward restitution and reconciliation. Obviously, the larger the community is, the more difficult this can be because of less cohesion and greater anonymity (factors that also contribute to our escalating crime rates). Perhaps that is why this worked so well in the past, when the state was less of a monolith and people were more connected, but that shouldn't deter a given population from attempting to think as a communal entity—especially since our faith insists that we are our brothers' keepers.

At the appropriate time the victim may wish to meet with the guilty party, although this is a difficult step that requires great sensitivity and expert mediation. Many victims are severely traumatized and may take years to come to this point. There are many grace-filled stories of meetings, though, like that of Anne Marie and her father's killer. Although her reconciliation was seventeen years in the making, others with a strong faith—like Mrs. Walker—are able to forgive and begin the healing process sooner.

It's too soon to tell if restorative justice programs are making a difference in the recidivism rates of criminals. But victims who have used them are effusive in their gratitude for the help they offer in moving on, and that's important.

It appears that the programs work because they inherently reflect the way that sin both offends the victim and sullies the dignity of the offender. They also recognize the greater communion that is disturbed with each sin, which should be addressed as a part of the healing process. While secular programs will not call these crimes "sins"—nor will they call the criminals to repent for their offenses against God—as long as Christian chaplains have access to the prisons and carry this excellent work forward, that dimension will not be lost.

Justice and God
Only God is perfectly just, and thus the justice of God is not something that we should ever appeal to lightly, "since all have sinned and fall short" (Romans 3:23). Furthermore, if justice is applied according to what is due to the other, Christians cannot simply measure out what we find to be fair or evenhanded, for that is not what God has taught. We owe God our love because he is love. We honor him in our religious observances and in the way we respond to our neighbor who is made in his image. There is no escaping this—even in our recourse to justice.

Msgr. Robert Hugh Benson cautioned us not to tie our work of forgiveness to the worthy quest for justice:

> …We must not wait until wounded pride is made whole by the conscious shame of our enemy; until the debt is paid by acknowledgment and we are complacent once more in the knowledge that justice has been done to us at last. On the contrary, the only forgiveness that is supernatural, and which, therefore, alone is meritorious, is that which [reaches] out to men's ignorance and not their knowledge of their need.[40]

In this light the worldly justice behind which we may want to take refuge falls short, for its balance sheet ignores the founding principle on which it is ultimately based: the divine essence. Given the inseparable relationship between justice and love, then, it is actually justice itself that demands us to forgive our neighbor all things—under all circumstances and in every encounter—and to apply all punishments with care.

CHAPTER FIFTEEN

The Law of the Gift

But God, who is rich in mercy, out of the great love with which he loved us, even when we were dead through our trespasses, made us alive together with Christ (by grace you have been saved), and raised us up with him, and made us sit with him in the heavenly places in Christ Jesus, that in the coming ages he might show the immeasurable riches of his grace in kindness toward us in Christ Jesus. For by grace you have been saved through faith; and this is not your own doing, it is the gift of God—not because of works, lest any man should boast. For we are his workmanship, created in Christ Jesus for good works, which God prepared beforehand, that we should walk in them. (Ephesians 2:4–10)

Many may find this chapter difficult—even impenetrable—and I suggest that it be skipped until at least some work has been done in the realm of forgiveness. The challenge to let go of our injuries is monumental enough, and the suggestion that one might go further to see the injuries in another light may appear absurd. This is understandable, but if shards of light have already come through your dark landscape—showing you that there is a world on the other side of forgiveness—perhaps you may understand what follows.

God the Generous Giver

As creatures of God, we must learn to receive everything that we have as a gift. We begin with our very lives, which came from his benevolent hand. Although we came into being only at a given point in time, God saw each of us from all eternity and looked forward to our existence with great joy. That we are created in his likeness, sustained by his love, and directed to his eternal embrace is a gift. Sadly, in a jaundiced world immersed in myriad problems, this basic fact is often overlooked, but that makes it no less true.

There are many other things we should recognize as gifts beyond our own existence: harmony among family members, the kind actions of a loving spouse, the children entrusted to our care, a just employer, the opportunity to use our skills, civility in the workplace, and friends who share our worldview. We can certainly get used to these things, even if we technically know that Providence had something to do with them. How many times we've prayed for our children's health, or for the right job, or for our house to sell quickly, or for any number of good things and our prayers were answered. We may toss up a word of thanks but then move on to the next challenge attached to that home or job. It's only natural—we couldn't stay at a fever pitch of gratitude, could we?

Perhaps we need to spend some time thinking about our expectations, because the gratitude for these good things is often lost in the premise of our own goodness. This is reflected in the standard question that most people ponder at one time or another: "Why do bad things happen to good people?" As far as we have come in life, and even in this book, we've blithely shared the assumption that we are "good people." In this regard I have deliberately chosen to write on the premise that what has happened to you was undeserved. But was it?

On one level, of course, bad things are undeserved, unjust, and occasionally criminal. It is entirely fitting that we consider these actions as such, for no child deserves to be molested, no wife deserves to be abandoned, and no person deserves to witness the murder of loved ones. All of these transgressions fly in the face of charity; they are what God calls sin.

Sin was not supposed to be a part of our world, but it is. We deal with it every day—in ourselves and in others. We are all sinners who offend each other and God on a regular basis. As we consider our expectations, we must keep this fact in mind.

Although we have come to take good things for granted, we don't deserve them. Even so, Our Lord has seen fit to give us any manner of good things, beginning with his forgiveness. "While we were yet helpless, at the right time Christ died for the ungodly.... God shows his love for us in that while we were yet sinners Christ died for us" (Romans 5:6, 8). His gift of atonement for our depravity wasn't a divine decree from a lofty height; it was wrought in human flesh pinned to one of our own trees by means of forged iron nails. Our life came at the price of his death, given freely in the worst of circumstances. As much as we may come to love him, to appreciate his sacrifice, and to do what we can to spread his love, we will never be entitled to what he offers us.

So might there be another way to consider the bad things that happen?

In his biography of St. Francis of Assisi, G.K. Chesterton suggests an impossible exercise. Imagine, he says, that you could burrow into the earth until you came out on the other side. There would be a period in which you were going down, so to speak, but at a certain point—somewhere past the core—your downward journey would be a task of rising. Despite traveling on a single trajectory, you would no longer be moving away from the light but moving to embrace it. What that allegory cannot explain is how, in the Christian journey, the light regained is a thousand times more brilliant than what was left behind.[41]

Not only is the light more radiant, it is more deeply appreciated—along with the world now seen from a new perspective, which is what the trusting soul is invited to experience. As we meditate anew on the gifts we have been given, we soon discover that we should not come to expect them. In fact, if we wish to put on Christ—the Man-God who deserves all our love, gratitude, and adoration—then we will eschew those good things, giving them away entirely. Furthermore, we will begin to ask if the difficult parts of our life, even the worst events, have not also been gifts.

Detaching From Our Treasures

How do we give away our gifts? We begin by detaching from them in a human sense. They may remain entirely within our grasp, but our relationship to them changes.

To use our children as the first example, we place them on God's holy altar and entrust them entirely to his care. We understand that we don't own them—nor do we expect anything from

SET FREE

them other than what we owe to God on their behalf. When they act irresponsibly or lack appreciation, we don't look at the injury to ourselves, for we have no command over them. God, of course, wants them to be virtuous, which includes filial piety and acts of devotion. But we remove ourselves from the equation: Each deficiency is strictly between that child and God.

Janice had the sorrow of watching one of her children succumb to drug and alcohol abuse, which was wrenching to the entire family. Her daughter's behavior was increasingly insulting and depraved, and it was also an embarrassment in her small town. As Janice learned how to detach in love—which is essential to surviving this sort of tragedy—she regularly gave this "gift" back to God. She imagined heaving that dear child onto the altar of her local parish and stepping away, entrusting her future to God's most holy will. (There was nothing to be done anyway, since you cannot force another to be good.) This was her acknowledgment of a singular truth: Her daughter was God's precious child, entrusted to Janice in only a secondary way.

The transformation made life bearable in the long years until her daughter became clean and sober. Also transformed was her relationship with her other children. They too were only "on loan"; they were primarily in the care of a God who loved them infinitely more than Janice and her husband did.

In realizing that these children were souls being formed for an eternity with their Creator, Janice was able to let go of her own hurts in light of their shortcomings. Their insensitive words (yes, family life can be filled with them), their youthful self-absorption, and their immature myopia failed to rattle her; in many ways these concerns even failed to register. Janice was every bit as engaged—she loved her children and prayed for their souls as fervently as possible—but she learned to not take their actions personally. She gave all her children back to God, and she could appreciate any of their kind words and thoughtful deeds as undeserved treasures.

So we come to the life that is possible only when we give our gifts away. We must study this step in this book because of the impact it has on the work of forgiveness. Seeing this gift in the proper light directs the manner in which we offer it to others.

> Forgive, and you will be forgiven; give, and it will be given to you; good measure, pressed down, shaken together, running over, will be put into your lap. For the measure you give will be the measure you get back. (Luke 6:37b–38)

Since there are no limits to Christ's gifts, there should be no limit to our own—even in this difficult work. For what gift can compare to the Passion offered on our behalf?

Whereas the technical details surrounding forgiveness were previously explained (naming the injury, grieving the wound, making the act of forgiveness, and confessing residual resentments), we now come to a way of life that changes the whole landscape—that will actually make much of the hard work unnecessary. If we make sure that God increases and that we decrease (see John 3:30), then we short-circuit the need to forgive, for we deflect the disappointments that are attached to our unwieldy expectations. We are capable of a spiritual maturity that recognizes our own littleness and the littleness of others.

Just as a mother wouldn't become personally offended over her two-year-old's tantrum (although she would discipline the child appropriately), a mature woman who understands forgiveness shouldn't be personally offended when a poorly formed coworker insults her or a neighbor neglects to thank her for a painstaking act of charity. Do we not insult God regularly? Do we ever thank him enough for his favors?

People who are incapable of living virtue are diminished, and God's image in them is sullied. Rather than licking our own wounds, how much more should we console him for any disappointment over his scorned graces, while keeping before our eyes the painful truth that we have disappointed him greatly ourselves.

Suffering Is Also a Gift

When we reach this level of spiritual health, as paradoxical as it may sound, we will begin to receive our injuries as gifts. Yes, they are offenses against God, they undermine the dignity of the ones who inflicted them, and they are not a part of the perfect plan of God, but they are nevertheless gifts. They are opportunities to share in the suffering of Christ—the ultimate victim of every transgression—and they cause us to grow in ways that we would not otherwise grow. They remind us of the darkness of sin and the reasons that we should not act likewise.

Finally, if we tend toward the mercenary, the more we bear in a loving manner here on earth, the less we will suffer in purgatory. If we accept the reality of a sinful world, then this resigned—even cheerful—attitude helps us avoid shock or frustration over the fact that we wound one another regularly.

While this could be construed as "lowering the bar," it could also be understood as readjusting our vision and aligning our expectations according to the way things are. To be sure, we were truly made for love, and God wants our families to exude gladness and mutual respect. Every injury is grievous—committed by a child of God, wounding a child of God, and rejecting the perfect will of God. But the beauty of our incarnate faith is that each transgression can be embraced for its relation to Our Lord's own passion.

If we detach in love, overcoming our fears of being hurt by the actions of others, then we will have another level of freedom to extend ourselves generously as the gospel commands. We will no longer have to contort ourselves to love only in avenues where we are reasonably assured of a positive response, because all the responses are God's alone. Only then can we begin to understand the very ways of God. Jesus said,

> But I say to you, Love your enemies and pray for those who persecute you, so that you may be sons of your Father who is in heaven; for he makes his sun rise on the evil and on the good, and sends rains on the on the just and on the unjust. (Matthew 5:44–45)

This transformation is available to all who wish to persevere in forgiveness, enabling them to dredge up old wounds and peel off layer after layer of the complex interactions. As a woman discovers that the associated traumas are healed and that the freedom outweighs her fears, she can go deeper and deeper into the Sacred Heart, which was pierced on our behalf. Delving into that gift should put all the rest in perspective, as seeing our part in his suffering is a sobering reminder of how very little we deserve. As Chesterton remarked, "He who has seen the whole world hanging on a hair of the mercy of God has seen the truth, we might almost say the cold truth."[42]

But fully aware of this, as we become littler and more humble, his infinite, tender love will carry us forward into our undeserved heaven of consolations.

> As it is written,
> "What no eye has seen, nor ear heard,
> nor the heart of man conceived,
> what God has prepared for those who love him."
> (1 Corinthians 2:9)

Do we love him this much yet? And are we capable of loving our enemies this much, who also bear his image and likeness, who are more his than ours? This is the supreme challenge, and only those who are strengthened in the art of forgiveness will be capable of this sort of love.

It is upon these very souls that this world depends. This is integral to our vocation as living icons of Holy Mother Church. For the Church is essential in making our merciful Lord manifest. Indeed, she was born from his pierced side, as his tormented flesh gave life to the world.

CHAPTER SIXTEEN
The Divine Mercy

We couldn't close this study of forgiveness without considering its relationship to the Divine Mercy—a profound and urgent topic at this stage of salvation history. The twentieth century stood witness to unprecedented suffering, which included two world wars, innumerable other international conflicts, genocide of staggering proportions, gulags, atomic bombs, and the unspeakable horror of abortion. Man's love affair with technology allowed him to set his sights on those he feared and annihilate them.

And yet God continues to pour out his love because that is his essence, his nature, his very being. Is there no limit to what he will forgive? Evidently not, for he promised as much. In the midst of that bloody century, he emphasized his abiding love to a young Polish nun, Sr. Faustina Kowalska, in messages from 1931 to 1938.

Our Lord visited St. Faustina in her convent. He stressed that his mercy and kindness are always at the disposal of all people—especially those who suffer—and he pointed to the gift of his passion and death as proof of his desire that we be freed from the consequences of our sins. That gift stands for all time. Our intensified depravity in recent decades hasn't overridden his offer. In fact, the greater our propensity for self-destruction, the more radical, the more astonishing, is his healing.

The healing was offered through repentance in the Old Testament, as Isaiah stated:

> Wash yourselves; make yourselves clean;
>   remove the evil of your doings
>   from before my eyes;
> cease to do evil...
>
>   ...
>
> Come now, let us reason together,
>   says the LORD:
> though your sins are like scarlet,
>   they shall be as white as snow;
> though they are red like crimson,
>   they shall become like wool (Isaiah 1:16, 18).

What could be starker than the difference between crimson and white?

How is this possible? We need to consider some theological truths. Recall that in the opening chapters of this book, we outlined the nature of God: He is pure "being" and total love. Let's compare love before the Fall and afterward.

Before creation God was completely happy in himself, as the three Persons of the Trinity lived in a perfect, eternal embrace of love. Even as creation unfolded, that divine love emanated outwards in a heady rush, filling everything with its goodness and beauty. When sin entered the world, its "nonbeing" was a tragic *no* to that goodness, a freely chosen rejection of God's essence. God honored the free will of humans, despite the rebellion that ensued. As the Church has long taught, God permits evil in order to draw from it a greater good (see CCC, 309–314).

The consequences of sin allow us to understand more about the order and justice of God and also add to our understanding of his love. When a person bears love for that which is perfect, it is simply love; but when love embraces that which is imperfect, it includes mercy—a forbearance that wasn't previously necessary. Our intransigence didn't change God—he is immutable—but through it we learned that the love intrinsic to his nature includes an unquenchable mercy, which does not shrink from us even in our corrupt state.

Is There Really a Greater Good?

Let us take the Old Testament story of Joseph—the young man sold into slavery by his own brothers. Joseph was one of the younger sons in a large family in which there had been multiple wives, and he happened to be his father's obvious favorite. This occurs occasionally, even when children are not in stepfamilies but share the same parents. Sometimes it's because of particular physical characteristics; sometimes a parent favors boys over girls (or vice versa); and sometimes favoritism is related to a child's temperament. In Joseph's case it was because his mother was a beloved wife. No matter the reason, it's all too common within families, and children feel the inequality keenly.

Jacob gave Joseph a beautiful coat, which further irritated his brothers. To make matters worse, Joseph paraded about, flaunting the gift. In response, the brothers plotted to murder him but then changed their minds, instead selling him as a slave to a passing caravan.

At this point there are myriad sins that have contributed to a reprehensible decision: the unequal love of the father, the preening of the son, the jealousy of the brothers, and the unsavory trading in human flesh. None can be justified, for each element harms a neighbor, degrades the sinner, and weakens the bonds of communion within families and the greater society.

Joseph suffered more transgressions against him in Egypt. Temptation, entrapment, and perjury led to his arrest. And yet his gift of reading dreams brought him to the attention of the Pharaoh, who put him in a position of tremendous authority. That status and the attendant success allowed him, years later, to save his starving kinsmen—the very ones who had treated him so badly.

That is one example of the mystery that we repeatedly encounter: God can transform something that is scarlet into that which is whiter than wool. That which is objectively evil can lead to great good.

The Divine Mercy permeates every layer of Joseph's story, as it does our very own. We have been jealous, we have lied, we have misused our gifts, we have exploited others for our own benefit, we have sinned in our imagination, and we have languished far from God—bewailing our miserable fates. And yet, if we will forgive as Joseph did, we can cast off the power of darkness and be welcomed back into the light.

The Implications for Us

As we deepen our understanding and appreciation for the love of God, it will have two implications for us who are in his image and likeness and called to love as he loves. First, we must consider the end for which we are made. Our only purpose for existing is to love God in this life and to live with him for eternity. To that extent, our very life is already wrapped up in his, because our very being is contingent on his perfect being. Our being makes no sense apart from God.

When we sin, we diminish our very being and risk damnation. When our intellect isn't ordered to the truth or our will isn't directed to what is good, we rebel against God, who is both truth and goodness. We are made for communion: There is a gravity in God that pulls us to him. But sin cannot be a part of that communion.

The amazing thing about sin—"nonbeing"—is that when it is forgiven, it really is obliterated.

> He does not deal with us according to our sins,
>   nor repay us according to our iniquities.
> …
> [A]s far as the east is from the west,
>   so far does he remove our transgressions from us.
> (Psalm 103:10, 12)

As far as the east is from the west? That infinite analogy means it is gone, for our good God will not dwell on a negative. (The only reason sin mattered to him before our repentance is that it was attached to something that he loves passionately: our souls!) Thus, though its rippling effects may continue in the mundane order, the sin itself ceases to exist, and the heavens exult. "Just so, I tell you, there will be more joy in heaven over one sinner who repents than over ninety-nine righteous persons who need no repentance" (Luke 15:7).

That brings us to the second point, which concerns the way that we love. As noted in the first chapter, the essence of our vocation is to love, and the particular way that women love is as icons of Holy Mother Church. That means there is an all-encompassing maternity to the way that we receive the human person, and we are called to a profound spousal unity with God. Now we see that the love we bear must include mercy, for that is the way that God loves. As God shows mercy in loving each of us, we extend that life-giving gift in the mercy that we show to others. Indeed, the greater the depravity, the more miserable the sin, the more gracious and sweeping should our mercy be.

On our own, of course, this is impossible, but we are not extending our own mercy. We are simply passing along the gift he offers, which is infinite. It is who he is, and thus as we contemplate him in the intimacy of our prayer, through the Communions we receive and in the graces he offers, we will come to a greater understanding that this is—by extension—who we are called to be. If we consider the love of God to be like a magnet, drawing us toward him, then we might recognize that the sins we bear repel that force; they counteract the very gravity of his existence, which draws us into union with him. As we forgive those who trespass against us, we jettison that which holds us back—allowing a deeper intimacy with God.

And yet, as helpful as the idea of a magnet may be, we're not dealing with an abstract source of energy. We are dealing with persons—both the divine person of God and the finite persons he has created (and that includes the difficult persons with whom we interact daily!). The beauty of the new translation of the liturgy is that it restores in many of its prayers the image of God's face, which is an anthropomorphic idea that reminds us that he is not a force but a lover. And the only limit on his love is our human freedom—the very freedom that allows our corresponding love to be authentic.

The tremendous love God bears for my soul is matched by the corresponding love for every other soul, and thus the communion he offers creates a bond among us, so that we can be drawn as a body into his own. Lest this notion be confused with non-Christian ideas of union, it is essential that we remember that our personhood will ever remain distinct, and our integrity will always be maintained. He would never annihilate the ones he loves. Even our call to humility isn't meant to erase us—only those elements of pride that distort the reality of who we really are.

God's mercy was borne to the world by means of his humility, and his love reached down to offer the supreme act of forgiveness. Will we respond if the price he asks is our own forbearance of the sins of others? Can we stoop to absorb the injustices we suffer, as Christ did? Can we create bridges of communion by casting off the evil that seeks to isolate each soul in darkness? Will we join our suffering to that of Jesus and his Blessed Mother, who each bore tremendous pain for the greater good?

These are the questions we need to take to prayer as we consider our call to forgive. God's own Divine Mercy is our model, and Our Lady was the first disciple. There is no other path to unity with God, no other way to authentic peace in this life, and no more perfect way to align our being with Being itself. In showing mercy, we are our best selves, the persons God created us to be.

When Joseph forgave his brothers and reunited with his family, they were all fed despite a great famine. His thorough act of forgiveness held off death itself, and their love renewed was a wine richer and sweeter than unpressed grapes could have offered. Using our freedom and our will to forgive others is a gift. When sifted through God's hands, it will bear more fruit than we could ever imagine.

CHAPTER SEVENTEEN

Forgiveness Brings Freedom

This work has tried to explain the theological case for forgiveness and to make it clear that our salvation hinges on doing as Our Lord commanded. It also presents another compelling reason to forgive those who have harmed us: Apart from the religious mandate, forgiveness offers the path to peace of mind and freedom to live the fullest expression of our human dignity.

While this may seem to comprise a separate motive, it is all of a piece. The same God who wants us to live with him for eternity in joy and bliss has created us for freedom now, and his divine precepts are meant for our own good during this challenging sojourn on earth. Ultimately we are the ones who benefit from this practice of forgiveness.

Freedom and Prudence

One point of confusion attached to the concept of forgiveness arises from the Christian understanding that suffering should be endured patiently. This leads many to believe that being holy means being a doormat for bad people. While suffering and patience are both essential to our journey, they cannot be embraced apart from the prudence that guides them.

Prudence is one of the four "cardinal" virtues, which means that it is a "hinge" on which other virtues depend.[43] The

Catechism explains that prudence enables us to make healthy choices:

> *Prudence* is the virtue that disposes practical reason to discern our true good in every circumstance and to choose the right means of achieving it.... It is called *auriga virtutum* (the charioteer of the virtues); it guides the other virtues by setting rule and measure. It is prudence that immediately guides the judgment of conscience. The prudent man determines and directs his conduct in accordance with this judgment. With the help of this virtue we apply moral principles to partic-ular cases without error and overcome doubts about the good to achieve and the evil to avoid. (*CCC*, 1806)

Prudence should undergird the choice of a life partner and a job, the sound raising of children, and the care of one's extended circle. When a person is in a state of grace and free from bitter-ness and resentment, she can see her way clear to each decision. The more practiced she is in applying Christian principles to her everyday life, the more naturally prudence will guide her as circumstances arise. In this regard it is easy to see how God's authority is ordered to our peace of mind.

Prudence helps a woman distinguish when to remain in a hostile environment and when to leave, when to bear with the unkindness of others and when to avoid being an enabler. Consider the bitter woman who is tied to an abusive partner by her low self-esteem and lack of options. In this trapped state the daily injuries that accrue spiral into one enormous ball of pain. The anger beneath the surface often flares up, even bordering on rage. The end result is that both parties are crushed under the weight of sin.

But it may interest readers to know that Helen, who forgave her abusive stepfather, Stan, was healed enough to nurse him in his final illness. Despite the brittle marriage between her mother and Stan, his lack of self-awareness, and the absence of any apologies from either him or his wife, Helen could fulfill her filial duties to them both in a cheerful manner. This was clearly possible only through God's grace. While a bitter woman might succumb to inertia, Helen chose to serve in total freedom.

Sometimes it may be difficult to distinguish from the outside the difference between forgiveness and enabling, but the two attitudes are utterly foreign to one another. Not everyone is capable of such valor, but the one who is called to heroic sacrifice learns to deflect bitter arrows with ongoing acts of forgiveness and confession and with a maternal heart disposed to offer God's own love to the unlovable. Helen's transformation did indeed "renew the face of the earth"—at least her little portion of it. And it was prudence that sustained her.

When forgiveness becomes habitual, one can rely on prudence to illuminate how to proceed even in the most delicate circumstances. Interestingly, it's not necessarily the choice but the disposition of the one making the choice that makes the difference. Two women in similar circumstances may discern different responses, while the same choice made by two women may be an occasion of sin for one and a path to sainthood for the other. That is why, in the introduction to this book, I insisted that I don't know what the right choice for another may be. In pretending otherwise I could trample on the Holy Spirit, who does know the best choice in each circumstance.

Freedom and Love

As outlined in chapter one, the heart of the feminine vocation is bridal love, because each woman is called to live as an icon of Holy Mother Church. Love is the only perfect use of our freedom. Despite the fact that it may require great sacrifice and often entails the risk of rejection, we must love. As icons of the bride, we know that we are to follow the Bridegroom and to imitate him.

We already know that he will take us with him to the cross, where we will be invited to transform our lives through an oblation of self. That oblation will come through the trials of the world, the very trials that have the potential of purifying and refining us if we unite them to his suffering. We know by faith that the union we seek requires that we forgive. Only then do we become free to love without fear.

The choice is not between a pain-free life without God and a life of tribulation with him. The suffering will come regardless of our decision about Jesus. The choice is whether to transform the inevitable struggles or to live a half-life—of either anxiety anticipating the pain or being consumed by that which we can't evade. The entire paradox of the Christian life is that we are called to love, to suffer, to forgive, and to find joy in that which is. Only then are we caught up in Being itself.

Forgiveness will alter our hearts, and that is the secret to loving with abandon. The alteration doesn't just fortify our hearts; nor does it build calluses so that they feel less. Quite the opposite. The transformation that Christ offers us—through loving fearlessly, despite the tears and trials—is nothing less than the opportunity to divinize our hearts.

The Call to Glory and Excellence

We come to the pinnacle of the Christian life, which is union with God. The remarkable truth about the God of mercy—who wants us to love with his love—is that he extends himself to his cherished souls more intimately than we can imagine. As shown earlier, all good inspirations originate in him, and all our good works are his works. What we need to absorb is the more extraordinary truth: that when we act in concert with his will and extend his compassion and forbearance to the world, we actually internalize him to the degree that our hearts become his dwelling places. With our permission God will not only exchange our hearts of stone for hearts of flesh (see Ezekiel 36:26) but also elevate them into his very glory (2 Corinthians 3:18).

This is not the self-divinization that Eve tried to grasp in the garden but the gift of God through baptism and a life lived fully open to the Spirit. God the Father is its source, and it came to the world through Mary's *fiat*. As St. Peter explains:

> His divine power has granted to us all things that pertain to life and godliness, through the knowledge of him who called us to his own glory and excellence, by which he has granted to us his precious and very great promises, that through these you may escape from the corruption that is in the world because of passion, and become partakers of the divine nature. (2 Peter 1:3–4)

All that we have endured up to this point has not been an obstacle to God, but rather an entrée for him to work more profoundly in our lives. A wise Dominican, Jean Corbon, speaks of a "liturgy of the heart" in which the soul reaches out for communion with its Creator. At one particular moment the hand of the priest—the *alter Christi*—is extended over our gifts, our wounded hearts that we hand back to God to heal: "The epiclesis on the altar of the heart must be intense at these moments, so that the Holy Spirit may touch and consume our death and the sin that is death's sting."[44]

What is this death of which he writes, since it doesn't imply our final end? It's the self-emptying that comes when we let go of the old life and wait for Christ to renew us with his own, as Romano Guardini explains: "Between the states of sinfulness and sinlessness lies a death, a destruction in which the sinner is submerged, in order to be lifted from it into a new existence."[45] This is the deepest mystery of our faith, the inscrutable truth whereby sin and death can be eradicated by the blood of the Lamb. Not only do we prostrate ourselves in grief, but we reach out to Christ, and his Easter becomes our Easter.

As icons of the Church, whose spirit is the Holy Spirit, we must love with God's heart—which is infinite mercy itself. Our motherhood is lifted into the Trinitarian realm, where our children are loved into eternity by the Father who gave them to us in the first place. This is the reality of the Incarnation, which invites the flesh into communion with the Spirit, who will always sustain us if we but ask.

Surely we can be tempted to reject such an offer, to compromise out of the fear that this is too good to be true. The fallen angels ardently wish for us to miss the opportunities for grace and healing. We must look to the saints and imitate their example, as St. Paul adds: "What I have forgiven, if I have forgiven anything, has been for your sake in the presence of Christ, to keep Satan from gaining the advantage over us; for we are not ignorant of his designs" (2 Corinthians 2:10b–11).

Knowing the enemy, and knowing the power of God over that enemy, we must trust in the power of forgiveness. Trust the amazing stories offered to you in the preceding chapters, and trust the promises of God. Let go of the burdens you carry— including those that have disguised themselves in different ways. You are not a victim but a beloved child of God and one he anxiously waits to console and heal. The liberation that lies ahead will be a source of joy, and there is no limit to the graces attached.

Jesus was clear in the prayer he taught us: We ask God to "forgive us our trespasses as we forgive those who trespass against us." What begins as an act of the will—in imitation of his divine mercy—ends with the sweetest of consolations, as he transforms our Gethsemane into a garden of delights through the power of love.

The women who are contemplating how to begin the work of forgiveness should not be distracted by the larger implications—their personal healing is paramount! But those who have already accomplished some steps and are finding "the tranquility of order"[46] that comes accrues therein may want to consider those very things.

The precarious state of our society at the opening of the twenty-first century adds urgency to the message of this book. The vociferous public battles over religious liberty and sexual morality have revealed that there is a yawning rift in the American population—not only between those who understand the Constitution and those who don't but also between those who consider Christian virtue to be an essential element of our cultural fabric and those who reject it out of hand. Ongoing discussions make it clear that many people have a disparaging view of authority and a withering attitude toward the Church in general.

As distressing as it is to hear the angry voices, we must conclude that a country that countenances the killing of millions of babies, that has such a deeply confused understanding of marriage that it is attempting to legally redefine it, and that refuses to differentiate between virtue and vice in the formation of its children is very, very far from God. Furthermore, if the stories included in this book are any indication of the personal devastation that each sin causes in the souls it touches, then a society that includes such depravity must be populated with a great number of wounded individuals.

If people are not brought to the healing that forgiveness provides, we must conclude that the moral dissolution will only intensify. For without the contrition and reparation that each sin requires, we can neither choose wisely nor legislate justly. As St. Paul warns us, "The wages of sin is death" (Romans 6:23). The wages of manifold obstinacy and resentment in our midst has been the "culture of death" that we see today.

> The fear of the LORD is the beginning of wisdom;
>   a good understanding have all those who practice it.
> (Psalm 111:10)

So said King David, and indeed his knowledge of God led to heartfelt repentance over his own sins. That repentance is what we need at this point in history, and it begins with each of us. As each woman considers her obligation before God to acknowledge her sinfulness, and subsequently to forgive those who have trespassed against her, she can begin to live the fullness of her spiritual maternity in freedom and love.

We must summon the very heart of the Bridegroom's message, which was integral to St. Thérèse's "little way." She reminds us that "Jesus looked with merciful love at those who had wounded his hands and his feet, because those wounds were the very doors to heaven—even for those who had made them."[47] The acceptance and full embrace of this key truth will allow the authentic Catholic woman's gifts of prudence and wisdom to grow and deepen and thereby magnify the light of Christ to those around her. Thus she contributes her part "to aid mankind in not falling."[48]

Renouncing Curses

Tremendous freedom comes from the act of forgiveness, but another tool may be necessary when curses have been uttered. Curses are more than just insults or blasphemous invectives; they are words that call down evil on others. They can indeed bind others in a false sense of reality.

Family members and teachers can curse the little ones in their care even without knowing it, such as when criticisms they intend for instruction are composed of crippling words. For example, a mother who is unhappy with the state of her daughter's bedroom might say things like, "You never clean up after yourself," and, "You are such a mess." Both of these comments are curses, although the mother may mean well. The child might take her at her word and henceforth never clean up after herself.

The positive response is to distinguish between the room and the child. One can manage a comment like, "This room is unacceptable / a wreck / a horror." (Yes, we've all seen it!) And a calm, recollected mother might have the presence of mind to say, "You're capable of doing much better. Try again."

Surely we've all lost our tempers and said the wrong things, and we should apologize for disparaging words. This can also help us feel compassion toward those who harmed us when we were young. But the problem goes beyond imprecise language.

While we must forgive those who neglected to care for us as we deserved, we must also renounce the curses when we discover them—usually when we carefully sift through old memories—and replace them with blessings.

This is an important lesson in the popular novel *The Help*. The kindly Christian maid, Aibileen, is deeply concerned about the unrelenting curses laid on her little charge, Mae Mobley. She resolves to speak words of blessing daily to counter the bitter words of the child's mother. She believes that her own constant doses of "You kind, you smart, you important" will free the little girl from lasting psychological harms.[49]

The story of Jacob and Esau is instructive here. When Jacob used subterfuge to appropriate Isaac's blessing—a blessing that was Esau's birthright—they all knew that it couldn't be undone. Instead of asking that his father revoke the blessing, all Esau could do was ask if his father had another blessing to bestow on him (see Genesis 27).[50]

While curses have a limited amount of power, they are easily cast off by invoking the name of Jesus or by calling on his blood to wash them away. It is a simple prayer of deliverance, through which the verbal harm that was brought to bear on the victim is sundered by the power of the cross.

At their core curses are lies. Given what we know about God's tremendous love for every soul, any words of condemnation or suggestions that personal defects are insurmountable are false and even blasphemous. As St. Thérèse might say, "It is to limit a mercy which has no limit. It is to doubt the patience, the indulgence, the untiring clemency of Jesus."[51] We should all be attentive to the words spoken around us, in order to isolate and eradicate the lies that seek to unsettle those we love.

We need to cast off this darkness and replace it with the light of truth. For example: "I am a child of God, fully capable of cleaning my home." If the curse against you involved your very existence, such as, "I wish I'd never given birth to you," or, "If you had only been a boy," it may take heroic strength to verbalize the counterbalancing truth, but perhaps a friend can say to you, "God has delighted in your very life," or, "God saw you from all eternity as his precious daughter." Friends are invaluable in restoring our proper equilibrium.

Prayer and circumstances will determine our actions toward the one who curses us or others. One determined woman stopped her mother mid-sentence and demanded that she take back her words, but persons who cursed us in the past may no longer be part of our lives. What is important is that the lie be renounced, the curse be countered with an appropriate blessing, and the guilty party be forgiven from the heart.

Holy Hours of Reparation

The Holy Hour devotion originates from Our Lord's words in the Garden of Gethsemane—the place where his anguish caused him to sweat blood in anticipation of his passion. His suffering was twofold, for in his omniscience he was entirely aware of the minute details of the approaching horror and of the many beloved souls who would reject his gift of self.

Upon rising from his prayer, he found that those he had brought with him—Peter, James, and John—had not remained vigilant.

> And he came to the disciples and found them sleeping; and he said to Peter, "So, could you not watch with me one hour? Watch and pray that you may not enter into temptation; the spirit indeed is willing, but the flesh is weak." (Matthew 26:40–41)

Usually a proper Holy Hour is spent before the Blessed Sacrament, combining formal and informal prayers of praise and petition. There are indulgences attached to this devotion, and the graces that flow from it are abundant. For the sake of our work here in the realm of forgiveness though, perhaps another sort of Holy Hour can be attempted, one that combines our faltering good will with God's great desire to provide us with the necessary means to heal. In this form we offer particular hours of work and sacrifice for ourselves and those who have hurt us.

Consider the little indulgences we count on during the day—such as sundry snacks, checking e-mail and favorite websites, and sitting down to enjoy a movie or book. Perhaps these gratifications can be delayed one short hour. While one might be overwhelmed at the thought of a day without coffee, it may be manageable to delay that first sip. The same goes for the other little pleasures we count on. They offer opportunities for self-mastery and showing our desire for healing.

Another approach is to offer an hour's worth of work for a particular person. We might harbor deep anger at a parent or abusive friend, but sixty minutes of laundry or an hour of cleaning for that person's intentions can go a long way toward burning through the residual pain, making possible the act of forgiveness.

Our Lord knew that "the spirit indeed is willing, but the flesh is weak." In all honesty, many hours may be necessary, but the net result will be a purification of the soul, more ready grace from which to draw—and a cleaner house to boot!

For those who are not suffering an injury but know someone who is, offering sacrifices on her behalf can be an excellent way to participate in the healing process. Knowing that much of the world misunderstands this critical teaching—or finds it too hard—we might all remember to offer hours of self-denial for the worthy cause of enabling others to take their first steps toward God.

This creative adaptation of a Holy Hour cannot replace the time spent before Our Lord—the very Lord who taught us how to forgive while still in agony—but it is a good-faith effort toward making the right decision. The decision to forgive is a loving act of the will that mirrors his own and will restore our dignity in his likeness.

Kathleen Norris writes beautifully of the sacredness and cohesion of the most perfunctory of tasks:

> Laundry, liturgy and women's work all serve to ground us in the world, and they need not grind us down...they have a considerable spiritual import, and their significance for Christian theology, the way they come together in the fabric of faith, is not often appreciated.[52]

The same incarnational faith that saves us also reminds us of the sacramentality of work, which allows your Holy Hour to be joined to Christ's paschal gift. It doesn't matter where you are—whether you're in school, at work, or in the home. If the residual pain makes it hard to frame your intentions in pious language, then offer simple things throughout the day for your own healing, and how quickly you will find your heart transformed by divine love!

Resources

ACTS Missions is a ministry based in San Antonio, Texas. Retreats offered around the country focus on "Adoration, Community, Theology, and Service." For more information visit actsmissions.org

The Forgiveness Project is a charitable organization that explores forgiveness, reconciliation, and conflict resolution through real-life human experience. Based in the United Kingdom, it has no religious or political affiliations but freely shares its message in schools, prisons, and other community settings. It can be found online at theforgivenessproject.com.

The International Forgiveness Institute shares the healing message of forgiveness with both individuals and groups as a means of renewing society. It has created numerous forgiveness education curricula for children in war-torn, impoverished, and oppressed areas of the globe. Numerous books and testimonies are available at internationalforgiveness.com.

Made in His Image is an apostolate that seeks to help those who suffer from eating disorders through counseling in both outpatient and inpatient centers. It can be found online at ifight-himwithlove.wordpress.com/made-in-his-image/.

PACE is the Post-Abortion Counseling and Education program, which hosts a Scripture study of great help for those who have procured abortions.[53]

Rachel's Vineyard is a worldwide apostolate dedicated to bringing healing to those who have been harmed by abortion. The website is rachelsvineyard.org, and most diocesan Respect Life offices can provide a list of local retreats.

Prison Fellowship International's **Restorative Justice** ministry explores the communal impact of crime and seeks ways to repair communion after injury. More information can be found online at restorativejustice.org.

Twelve-Step Programs offer meetings that help those harmed by addictions, such as alcoholism and drug and gambling addictions. Some meetings are for the addict, and others are for those whose lives have been impacted by an addict; they are held at all times of the day and evening. Schedules, locations, and more information can be found at aa.org, al-anon/alateen.org, gamblersanonymous.org, and oa.org (Overeaters Anonymous).

An extremely helpful book has just been published by **Dawn Eden:** *My Peace I Give You: Healing Sexual Wounds With the Help of the Saints* (Ave Maria Press, 2012).

1. Closing documents of the Second Vatican Council (Pope Paul VI's address to women).
2. *Mulieris Dignitatem*, 26.
3. *Mulieris Dignitatem*, 26.
4. Pope John Paul II, *Mulieris Dignitatem*, Apostolic Letter on the Dignity and Vocation of Women, 30, quoting *Gaudium et Spes*, Pastoral Constitution on the Church in the Modern World, 24, www.vatican.va.Cf. Luke 17:33.
5. Closing Documents of The Second Vatican Council, Pope Paul VI, Address to Women, December 8, 1965, www.vatican.va.
6. *Dives in Misericordia*, 3, Encyclical, November 30, 1980, www.vatican.va.
7. *Dives in Misericordia*, 4.
8. *Dives in Misericordia*, 4.
9. *Dives in Misericordia*, 9.
10. Since the actions of others will be the point of such delicate conversations, we might wonder if we run the risk of gossip. If the conversation remains principled and confidential and is ordered to restoring communion, there will be no sin against charity. Rather counsel is a valuable spiritual work of mercy.
11. It is important that both are free to speak forthrightly and that the subjects raised don't unsettle the wounded one to the degree that she cannot function properly. For difficult injuries she may want to arrange a weekend away, with someone tending to her family responsibilities. It's especially hard to unpack what has been carefully hidden for a long time. In fact, such issues may have to be approached piecemeal.
12. John Paul II, *Familiaris Consortio*, 21.
13. *Familiaris Consortio*, 21.
14. Reinhold Niebuhr, 1934.
15. *Familiaris Consortio*, 17.
16. *Familiaris Consortio*, 17.
17. John Clarke, o.c.d., trans., *Story of a Soul: The Autobiography of St. Thérèse of Lisieux, Third Edition* (Washington, D.C.: ICS, 1996), pp. 65–66. Italics in the original. Thérèse had the habit of slipping into the third person in her autobiography, which explains the first sentence.

18. Consider, in particular the Marian icons from the East. They traditionally come from artists whose deep prayer life allows their work to be windows into eternity.

19. *Dei Verbum*, 7.

20. Jean Jacques Rousseau believed that man was born good and was made evil by society. If society could be improved, he reasoned, then man would correspondingly improve. The lie in this thesis was proven after two centuries of applied Enlightenment ideals, culminating in two of the most horrific wars in history—not to mention concentration camps, gulags, and other atrocities.

21. Interestingly, she states firmly that forgiving the molester was far easier than forgiving the members of the Church. She understood the sick state of his soul that would lead him along his path of perversion, even his abuse of her kindness to prey on her loved ones.

22. Ignatius of Antioch, Letter to the Romans, 4.

23. C.S. Lewis, *Mere Christianity* (San Francisco: Harper, 2001), p. 199.

24. The "Post Abortion Counseling Education" program is used in many Christian churches across the country.

25. The "Adoration, Community, Theology and Service" retreat program is based in San Antonio, Texas, and can be found online at actsmissions.org.

26. Theresa Burke and Leslie Graves, "Why I'm Not Allowed to Experience Healing," www.rachelsvineyard.org, p. 3.

27. Burke and Graves, pp. 3–4.

28. Charles Kingsley, "Three Fishers," in Edmund Clarence Stedman, ed., *A Victorian Anthology*, 1837–1895 (Cambridge: Riverside, 1895).

29. As quoted by Mike Pflanz, "Wife of Victim of Tom Cholmondeley Says I Forgive Him," *The Telegraph,* May 9, 2009, www.telegraph.co.uk.html.

30. Eva Kor, http://theforgivenessproject.com.

31. "The Way of Fatima," pp. 8–9, www.stfrancismagazine.info. Fatima was martyred in August 2008 in Saudi Arabia.

32. The organization is the Commission for the Promotion of Virtue and the Prevention of Vice. Neglect of Islam or conversion to another faith is considered not only "vice" but a capital offense.

33. "The Way of Fatima," p. 9.

34. See http://www.stfrancismagazine.info/ja/Fatima%20of%20Saudi%20Arabia.pdf.

35. John Hardon, "The Justice of God," from a retreat given in December 1988 to the Handmaids of the Precious Blood, www.therealpresence.org.

36. " 'I forgive you,' mother tells racist thugs who killed son," *Telegraph*, 1 December 2005.

37. Meena Barwa, "Orissa: Raped nun forgives aggressors and recounts her sufferings," December 7, 2011, www.asianews.it.

38. Anne Marie Hagan, theforgivenessproject.com.

39. "What Is Restorative Justice?" www.justicefellowship.org.

40. Robert Hugh Benson, "Your sins are forgiven," from *Paradoxes of Catholicism* (Scotts Valley, Calif.: CreateSpace, 2012), p. 41.

41. G.K. Chesterton, *Saint Francis of Assisi* (New York: Image, 2001), pp. 65–66.

42. Chesterton, p. 70.

43. The four cardinal virtues are prudence, justice, fortitude, and temperance.

44. Jean Corbon, *The Wellspring of Worship* (San Francisco: Ignatius, 2005), p. 223.

45. Romano Guardini, *The Lord* (Washington, D.C.: Regnery, 1982), p. 151.

46. St. Augustine, *City of God* 19, 13,1, as quoted in CCC, 2304.

47. Jean C.J. d'Elbée, *I Believe in Love: A Personal Retreat Based on the Teachings of St. Thérèse of Lisieux*, Marilyn Teichert and Madeliene Stebbins, trans. (Manchester, N.H.: Sophia, 2001), pp. 8–9.

48. Pope Paul VI, Address to Women.

49. Kathryn Stockett, *The Help* (New York: Putnam, 2009), p. 189.

50. The story of Jacob and Esau is complex. Rebecca's machinations are curious, and the blessing that Esau eventually receives is actually a curse. But the relevant lesson for our purpose here is the theological implications of a blessing.

51. D'Elbée, p. 62.

52. Kathleen Norris, *The Quotidian Mysteries: Laundry, Liturgy and "Women's Work"* (Mahwah, N.J.: Paulist, 1998), pp. 76–77.

53. For further information, ask your local pregnancy counseling center or pro-life office for local list of contacts.